Homeless Bear

CLAIRE CAREY

THE CLOISTER HOUSE PRESS

First published in the United Kingdom in 2023 by
The Cloister House Press

ISBN 978-1-913460-52-5

Chapter One

❦

When I was a single young man in the military, I always tried to keep myself detached from any serious relationships. I know that I only wanted one true love, so being in a relationship didn't seem the sensible thing to do while working in the military, and I was never looking for anything serious as a young man. I loved my job and everything that goes with that: the team spirit, the challenges, the rewards, of course, and a good day's work. This was my life, and I loved it – all of it. Being a young man in the military, there wasn't any room for a relationship – not a serious one anyway. I wanted to work hard and play hard; fun, and plenty of it. Some of the women I went out with lost interest as soon as they found out about my military background; I suppose they were fearful of getting close to me and then I'd be gone, off back to the army. This would be the type of woman I would look for in the future. Having said that, there were always the women who only liked one-night stands. They were all over me like a rash because of my status; the status kind of suited them, and they looked at me as a bit on the side, someone they could use to cheat on their partners with, and nobody would find out because I would soon be gone. Plus they loved the thrill; the naughtiness turned them on. This kind of woman wasn't for me though; they were just big trouble.

Not that I was any angel as a young man. I slept with a

1

couple of older married women, but the guilt I felt the next day was never worth it. A few of my friends said I shouldn't think like that – if the women wanted to take the chance it shouldn't bother me. But I always look at everything from both sides, and if I had a partner and she was up to no good with another person behind my back I wouldn't like it, so I chose not to walk down that road anymore. I was once told by a relative to always travel down life's road straight so that if you get any problems you can always back up. Good advice in my opinion. Sleeping with somebody else's partner wasn't keeping me on a straight road. So, all the loose women had to find someone else to use, and more fool the person allowing themselves to be used. I wasn't being that person anymore now that I was older and wiser.

Life is full of problems without us knowingly creating them. That's just what my father did, and that's why I will not be making his mistakes. History will not repeat itself through me if I can help it. My father completely messed up his perfectly good life, and that's not going to happen to me.

After ten years' service, I started to think about settling down. I had money in the bank – enough for a good deposit for a decent two-bedroom house. So, with that in mind, I started to pay more attention to the women I noticed around me. I still had four years left in the military and another tour of Afghanistan, so nothing too serious yet just in case, but I was definitely on the lookout. When thinking about the type of woman that appealed to me, the most important thing was finding someone I got on with, and that I could chat to. A woman who was knowledgeable of the way of the world because someday I wanted to travel – except unlike during my army career I only planned to visit the protected and peaceful parts of the world. So, I was looking for a woman with both feet on the ground and a level head on her shoulders – that was most important to me.

Some of my friends were more into finding a trophy wife, but that wasn't what I was looking for. My natural mum was a trophy for my father, and look what happened to him. I was looking for a partner I could trust with my life, a soulmate, a woman who appreciates a nice home and a good meal. I'm a good cook and I love sitting down at the end of the day with a nice meal. That's how life was at Aunt Josephine's – she made sure no matter how good or bad the day was, we all sat at the table for dinner. Aunt Josephine is an excellent cook and made sure we all knew how to cook. I would say that dinner was one of the most important times in our house. Aunt Josephine would get us all involved with peeling the potatoes, chopping the onions, peeling carrots, laying the table, washing up – we were all involved. I was very lucky to have been brought up by Aunt Josephine and my brothers and sisters: my oldest brother Khan, then my oldest sister Vy, then my youngest sister May, and youngest brother Jon, and – the baby of the bunch – me, Sean. Aunt Josephine is the only mother that I've ever known, although she isn't my natural mum. My natural mum up and left when I was two years of age, leaving me with my father, who was incapable of looking after me properly. Social services got involved and they removed me from my father, and it was only when Khan stepped in that I was prevented from being adopted into another family. Khan is thirteen years older than me and although he resented our father for what he did, he loved me. Khan told me after the separation of Father and Aunt Josephine, every other weekend Khan, Vy, May and Jon would all stay over at Father's, where all their time was spent looking after me. Khan later told me, 'When the time came for us all to go home each time it got harder to leave you because we all knew our father wasn't looking after you properly.'

My brothers and sisters would always take me to the playground and do the things that my dad wouldn't spare his time to do. Vy told me the first job she would do after arriving at Father's would be to bathe me, because Father couldn't even do that. I cannot remember any of this, but I've seen all the photos they had taken of us all together at Father's. My father couldn't cook and didn't know how to use the washing machine. I'm thankful that I can't remember any of this. Khan had told me the whole story once I was old enough to understand. It was my siblings that made sure I didn't go into full-time care or get put up for adoption. They convinced their mother, Aunt Josephine, to adopt me, so that I would grow up with my brothers and sisters.

It must have been very hard for Aunt Josephine to take on a child almost three years of age, that her husband of twenty years had fathered with a woman half her age, but she never let me see any hurt it caused her. I haven't felt any resentment from Aunt Josephine, only love and support. The only resentment I did feel once was from my youngest brother, Jon. Jon is only six years older than me, and he remembered the day Father left to be with my natural mum. I cannot imagine how hard that must have been for Jon. Khan told me that Jon cried for weeks after. Jon never forgave our father. Even now, all these years later, Jon has trouble even talking to our father. To be honest, when I sit and think about it, I don't blame him. And I understand why he would've felt slight resentment towards me at different times. But we're cool now. In fact, we get on very well.

Aunt Josephine is a very well organised woman, smart and very attractive. She keeps the home immaculate and she's very old-fashioned in her ways, believing the mother's job is at home with the children and looking after the home. Why on earth would any man exchange all that in the hopes that he was going to keep a woman half his age happy? How I see it now that I'm old enough to understand is that my father had everything, and got carried away by his own self-importance, and that temptation of that single woman half his age must have made him feel like he was God's gift to women. He had it all – a good wife, four children – and left it all for a little jam tart. What a foolish man. He couldn't resist and couldn't do anything wrong, in his own eyes. He was so far up his own arse that he couldn't see the wood for the trees. Like I said, a foolish, foolish man. To have a beautiful wife who never stopped working to keep their children comfortable and their home immaculate, putting the most delicious food on the table every day ... How can a man have so much, then go and fuck it all up for a quick shag with a young girl? What a fool our father turned out to be, and a big disappointment to his children. Sometimes I feel embarrassed for him.

My natural mother fucked off after two years, leaving me behind. I don't even remember her. Apparently, she met another man with more money and a bigger house and his own business. He was older than Father, but this guy had just lost his wife to ill health and didn't have any children, so he was the perfect sugar daddy. She quickly left my father without saying goodbye: she left me with a babysitter and left him a written note. My father was devastated – not so much about her but about what he had given up for her, only to have her just walk out as if he were nothing. She had found bigger fish to fry, and she wasn't hanging about, not even for me.

Khan told me that our father tried very hard to get back with Aunt Josephine, but she wasn't taking any more chances with him, because Father had turned their nice happy life on its head, and it took Aunt Josephine two years to get the children back on their feet. The only good thing our father did when he left Josephine was that he never took anything; he went empty-handed, leaving us the house and all the money. Khan also told me that even though Father was having an affair with my natural mother, he didn't want to leave Aunt Josephine. When it all came out, he wanted to stay with her, but she couldn't stand the embarrassment of it all and packed his bags for him. The day Father left was terrible, Khan said. It was the coldest day of his life, he added. Being the eldest child, Khan must have felt the pain of all of the siblings, and he was old enough to have some idea of what was to come. In a matter of minutes, he went from a carefree teenager with the world at his feet to the man of the house.

'I felt so cold that I couldn't even cry,' he told me. 'After two years we had all struggled to cope without Father, but then once we were all kind of back on our feet, I convinced Mother to adopt you. Mother was very reluctant at first to even talk about you. Then, some time after, we all spoke about the possibility as a family, and we decided that we didn't want our baby brother growing up in a children's home, or being adopted by a stranger. That sentence alone was the turning point for Mother. For the next six months, she put her heart and soul into working with social services so that she could adopt you. Father had hinted long before to Mother a few times when he realised that he couldn't cope with you after your natural mother walked out. He wanted you to come and live with us and for Mother to take you in, but at first Mother wouldn't hear of such an arrangement.'

But then, Khan explained, Josephine spoke to all four children and understood how much they wanted me to grow up with them. Aunt Josephine would learn to walk on water if it was going to make her family strong and happy. So, Aunt Josephine set about adopting me, and Khan said within six months they were able to collect me from the care home. Khan explained to me that when they all arrived to collect me, I was sitting on my own playing with some toys in the corner of the playroom.

'You were on your own with a sad lonely look on your face,' he said. 'You were just like a little homeless bear. A very sad homeless bear who just needs some love and care. And up until that moment you were in all honesty a homeless bear. When you saw us all arrive, your face lit up and you were transformed back into Sean. You must have somehow known we were there to collect you. From that moment on we all knew that we had made the right decision. Even Mother had tears in her eyes. It was a moment that I will never forget, or any of us will forget. Just the same as when Father left us, it's a memory so strong that it never fades away. But in your case, it was a memory so happy that you never want to forget – a memory to cherish forever. This time the memory was the warmest feeling, a sense of real achievement which can overpower any rubbish memory. Mother had made arrangements with social services for us all to collect you on Saturday, so it was a moment that we all will never forget – a very special time. Mother has always been good at making the most of a situation, looking for something positive. Collecting you that day somehow brought us all closer together, including Mother. You felt like the good in a bad situation.'

'You were three years of age, so the timing was perfect. We could all play with you and help Mother to take care of you, and that we did with the greatest of pleasure. You somehow had a way of making us feel united again. And you were young enough not to be able to remember being in the children's home. There was a downside to Mother adopting you though: It forced us to recognise that our father wasn't a good person – he was a selfish man. I suppose when your father walks out, you hold on to anything you can so that you don't blame yourself for it, and we had all held on to the idea that your natural mother had stolen our father with her youth. But now we know the truth. Bottom line: Father isn't a decent man. He's a self-centred, selfish, selfish man. There is only one good thing about him, for some reason he has a conscience, and that would turn out to be the only part that didn't let him down. We had a roof over our heads that was paid for, and when he left Mother he left her enough money to set up her floristry business without going into debt. That we must all be truly thankful for. Father knows in his heart that he can never make it up to us, but leaving us with a roof over our heads was his way of saying sorry, I suppose. However, it's no compensation for not having a father when you need him.'

'After your first day at home with us, we all let go of part of our father, and he knew that as well because the first time he visited us after we moved you in, he couldn't even look at you. He didn't say much, and we all felt very embarrassed for him as well as furious, and he sensed it. The atmosphere in the house that day was so intense that it almost felt like the day he decided to leave us. He tried to make polite conversation, but all we did was play with you, which made it even harder for him. I will never forget seeing the guilt that was written across his face. He made his excuses and left. It took him around three months to return.'

'Adopting you was the best thing we could have ever done because you came to us at three years of age, and you were the distraction we all needed – especially our mother. You were like a ray of sunshine – you put life back into our home, you filled the big hole that Father had left, and you marked the end of a very disruptive part of our lives. We all couldn't wait to get back from school, and later from work, to see you, and you couldn't wait for us all to come home, for our house to be complete again. Mother made sure every day we returned home from school or work you had something to show us, like a painting or a drawing, or you had made little cakes or big cakes. When you made cakes, you always made sure there was enough for all of us. Mother put all your paintings up on the fridge door just as she had done with all of us. Mother loved you as much as we did. After a couple of weeks, you settled in so quickly, just like you had always been here. You were the best thing to happen to us after Father left, without a doubt. Mother made sure that you called her Aunt Josephine – honesty was the best policy. The last thing Mother wanted was to bring you up living a lie, even though legally she is your mother. Because Father and your natural mother gave you up to be adopted, Mother always wanted the truth on the table so that later in life there couldn't be any upsets within our family. Mother never intended to replace your natural mother. She just wanted to be a mother to you. We have all turned out to be very good independent adults, making sure we put the most important thing first – family. Mother had somehow made an example of our father without causing us any unnecessary stress. None of us wanted the same outcome as Father. He was a bad example, and we all knew it.'

Aunt Josephine never put Father down; she just never mentioned him much. She put all her energy into making sure we were all happy and focused – focused on our life, focused on school, focused on our after-school clubs, focused on looking after our beautiful home, focused on making sure everything in our home was clean and tidy. Aunt Josephine made sure we had everything that we needed, and our home was always well maintained. In our house, there weren't any leaking taps, and I never remember seeing a light bulb out. We all had our indoors jobs, like hoovering and cleaning, and we all had our outdoors jobs, like mowing the lawns, cleaning the guttering, washing the windows inside and out, sweeping the footpaths – and that included the public footpath outside our house. 'Focused' was Aunt Josephine's favourite word.

Even though I never called Aunt Josephine 'Mother,' I never felt like she was anything except my mother. In truth, I felt like I could get away with not calling her Mother because I was the baby of the family. Sometimes, if I was feeling confident, I would drop the Aunt and my brothers and sisters would find this amusing.

*

I'd better introduce my siblings properly. Khan is a very thoughtful kind person who works as an electrician. Vy is a very quiet person. She loves law, and she has studied it ever since she could read, and prosecution is her thing. May is a very homely person who loves helping Aunt Josephine with the house and with her floristry. She likes to go shopping with her friends, and as soon as she was old enough she did voluntary work two days a week in a charity shop. She is very good at dressing the windows, so I suppose she is quite artistic, like Aunt Josephine with the floristry.

Jon is the rascal of the bunch and the clever one at the same time. He's always up to naughty stuff – but nothing that could get him into serious trouble because he's too clever for that. Jon is always late but never misses anything. He never likes his dinner, yet the plate is always empty. He didn't like school but he was at the top of the class. Everything seems to come easy to him. Jon is very intelligent and a builder by trade, specialising in designer buildings.

Then there is me, who is trying to learn something from each of my brothers and sisters. I'm more hands-on and didn't get on too well in school. Aunt Josephine signed me up for Scouts as soon as I was old enough, and I really enjoyed it. After Scouts I joined the army cadets, then the TA – that's the territorial army – and then finally I signed up for the army. For me, it was the best path to follow. I enjoyed the guidance, and it made me the strong man that I am today, which is something I wasn't sure I was going to become without a father figure. Aunt Josephine and my siblings never let me down, but you cannot help but wonder sometimes if things would have been different for me if my father had been there for me growing up. That's something I will never know. There is a very important lesson that I have learnt, and this is engraved on my heart: I know that I will never leave my children, not for anything or anybody.

*

My last move as a young man was Beachley barracks, just outside of Chepstow, so again it all seemed to fall into place for me. I was really happy in the Rifles first battalion. I spent fifteen years in the Rifles, saw some things I will probably never mention again, had some amazing experiences I never want to forget, and did some pretty rewarding stuff – and that is what it's all about. Without realising it until afterwards, joining the Rifles was my way of making sure I didn't turn out like Father. I wasn't selfish, and I wanted the world to know that.

Looking back now, Khan was the best father figure anybody could ever wish for. We were all lucky that Khan had a good head on his shoulders. Sensible, kind, caring and – best of all – reliable, Khan is definitely Aunt Josephine's son.

Father paid the price in the end after my natural mother left him: he suffered a breakdown followed by years of depression. He was never able to cope properly. Aunt Josephine wouldn't have a great deal to do with him, although she made sure he got treatment for the depression. As a young person, I often wondered why Aunt Josephine helped him with his depression, but now I realise that she hadn't wanted us children to go through any more unnecessary heartache. After years of not feeling well, he finally improved, but he was never quite the same again. Maybe it was partly down to him never having much social contact after the divorce. He told Aunt Josephine that he was embarrassed about his behaviour.

Like I said, there was only one decent thing about him – a conscience of sorts.

Getting involved with Fannie while married to Aunt Josephine was Father's biggest mistake. He really believed she loved him, and he was so flattered by her attention towards him, and she made him feel young again. If poison ivy was a person then Fannie was that person. Father told Khan the whole story because he wanted us all to know the truth so that we didn't get into the same mess – his conscience helping him out again.

'Fannie was like a bad drug and I was an addict,' Father told Khan. 'I was completely blinded by what was going on around me. She was all I could think about, and I had to have her. At first, she was my once-a-week fix, then we were meeting twice a week, and it soon turned into every day. Fannie didn't care where we met so long as she had my full attention.'

After about eighteen months of their affair, Fannie became pregnant with me. Father told Khan that he was shocked because they had been very careful. Father asked Fannie to have an abortion and she agreed, but by then Fannie was four months into the pregnancy and was advised not to have an abortion. This was a massive blow to Father because he knew that he couldn't keep his affair a secret any more. Father decided to tell Aunt Josephine about the situation he had put himself in, hoping she would help or support him – but there was worse to come for Father: Aunt Josephine is no fool, and she had already found out about the affair almost a year before Father had moved out. When she had found out, Aunt Josephine had moved out of the main bedroom and into the spare room, but Father was so enthralled with Fannie that he hadn't paid any attention to Mother sleeping in the spare room and assumed it was because of his snoring.

So by the time Father had finally built up the courage to tell Aunt Josephine about the affair, she had already done her homework on Fannie and found out that she was nothing more than a gold-digger looking for a sugar daddy. She decided that it was best if Father moved out to be with Fannie. Father was shocked by this stern approach, and by how calm she was. But she had enough time to think about the situation and time to plan. He asked if she was having an affair. Aunt Josephine was angry with Father for asking such a question. She told him, 'No. I have four children to look after. That's my only priority at this time.'

Aunt Josephine went straight upstairs and packed a bag for him. She advised him while she was packing the bag that he should go and explain to the children that he was leaving. Khan told me how all four of them somehow knew what was coming and were very sad, especially Jon, who begged Father not to leave. Vy and May were very upset but somehow managed to say calm. It was about a month after he moved out that he told Aunt Josephine that Fannie was expecting me. Again, Aunt Josephine already knew the situation because one of her friends worked in the family planning centre and told her about Fannie seeking abortion advice.

Aunt Josephine was perfectly calm about the situation.

'How can you be so calm?' Father asked.

'We have four children. One of us needs to be the adult and take responsibility for them. I don't want my children to suffer because you're too weak-minded. Fact is, one of us has to be grown up for the benefit of our four children.'

Then she asked if he had ever considered the impact all

this is going to have on the children. Father had no answer.

Khan believed that Father had never considered us or the impact it was going to have. He was just focused on himself. He wanted Fannie and believed he was entitled to her at whatever cost to his family. Father paid the price in the end. Khan said that he needed to be strong because he felt the weight of the family in the same way his mother did, and he wanted to make sure we all stayed focused in the same way Mother felt the importance of this, so that it had only a minimal impact on us all. I do believe that when she put the cards on the table like that, it made Father, for the first time, actually realise exactly what he had done, and maybe that was the start of the rift between Father and Fannie. I would say that was the first time Father realised he had been very foolish. I remembered the look on his face after mother told him.

After mother had straightened him up, putting him in his place, Fannie never got all her own way, because when he left he made sure that he left everything to us so that we always had a roof over our heads. When Fannie realised what Father had done, she knew that she would need a bigger fish to fry. Fannie never wanted a relationship; she just wanted a free meal ticket with extras.

Father told Khan, 'I have now realised that once Sean was born, she had a couple of other men on the go. Her phone never stopped. And she would be out for hours and tell me she was at the shop.'

The bottom line is my natural mother was a waste of space, and another person whose example I wouldn't be following.

So, looking back on my childhood I had a good upbringing, and for that I'm truly grateful, because my life could have been really tough with two selfish parents. I now believe that the key to a decent life is being sensible and straightforward – no bullshit or drama, unless, of course, you're planning to be on TV. And in case you are wondering, I've never seen my natural mother. She has never bothered with me at all, except for a birthday card every year with ten pounds in it. The cards are still in the envelopes, packed away. How I see things is that she was the vessel that brought me here and dropped me off, and I was very lucky that Aunt Josephine picked me up.

Chapter Two

❦

I was eighteen when I signed up for a military career. The training was tough and constant, but I was focused and determined, all thanks to Aunt Josephine. Once my training was completed it was time to really knuckle down and get stuck in, and that's just what I did. With my focused approach, I achieved all the goals that came my way. By the time I had ten years of service under my belt, I had become a very strong man, and a very confident man too.

I started to think about making a family of my own. When I was on leave, I always went and stayed with Aunt Josephine in my old bedroom. After a while, Aunt Josephine made plans to sell our family house so that she could downsize, and I realised that I would need my own place to live. Aunt Josephine assured me I could stay with her because she still had two bedrooms, and I was grateful to have that safety net, but I felt that it was time for me to have my own place. So, I started to look around and it wasn't too long before I found a lovely two-bedroom house in a beautiful little village just outside of Chepstow. There were peaceful open spaces, a playground, tennis courts, a village shop and post office, a local pub and a school – it was perfect. The house was a new build with a sizeable back garden. I was delighted and I wasted no time in buying it. No sooner had I stepped through the front door for the first time than Khan, Vy, May and Jon all arrived with Aunt Josephine. It was perfect. I couldn't have been happier if had won the lottery.

We had a housewarming party, and it was lovely to be all together again. Everybody managed to find a place to sleep. Khan's children set up tents in the garden because they wanted to have a camp-over. It was brilliant. My two-bedroom house felt like a mansion. We sat and talked until the early hours. The next morning Aunt Josephine, Vy and May went to the homewares store and bought me everything I needed – bedding, towels, cutlery and crockery, the lot. I went food shopping and filled up all the cupboards. Khan and Jon fitted a TV that Jon had bought me at a car boot sale. Then we all had dinner together. Spending the first couple of days in my new home with all my family was really special and I will anyways thank my lucky stars that I have such a caring, thoughtful family.

Once it was time for them all to leave, I felt sad. Even though there wasn't enough room for everyone, in all honesty, I still wanted them all to live with me. That night I got to bed, and I was so pleased with myself, so pleased with my new home. And I remember thinking to myself that all this was nothing without a family. That was going to be my next mission. I still had four years of service left, but I knew the time would pass quickly.

Two weeks in my new home and then I would be gone for four months. Back in time for Christmas, hopefully. I spent those two weeks moving in and organising my new home, doing all the little jobs, putting my mark on the place. I had made arrangements with my friend Paul

and his wife Sophie to stay at my house for the time I was away. They were having an extension built on their house, so they needed a place to stay for a few months, it was perfect for all of us: they helped me with the mortgage for the time they spent in my house, and they got somewhere comfortable to stay.

*

It was soon time for me to be back on duty. The four months I was away seemed to drag; I had never noticed time before when I was on duty. I believe it was because I couldn't help thinking of my plans for my new home. I imagined being in the house at Christmas. I was planning New Year's Day for all my family at my house. I was also thinking about buying myself a vehicle. All my thoughts now were for my future, and I started to feel my time in the military was coming to an end. I still had just over three years left, but that's nothing in the military because you are so busy most of the time. I also needed to think about what type of job I would like to do. I'm a hands-on person, so I couldn't work behind a desk. I was good at most tasks that had been handed to me. I had an HGV licence, I was a qualified welder, and I'd done plumbing jobs, and although I wasn't a qualified plumber I did quite like that job. All my plans were rattling around in my head, so maybe if I bought a vehicle I should consider a van. Oh, there was so much to think about. I decided to leave my plans aside for the time being and get on with the job at hand.

On my return home I had briefly forgotten about my new house. This was the first time I wasn't heading home to Aunt Josephine's house – I was heading back to my place, and that sounded very grown up. I couldn't wait to get to my place – this was a new feeling for me. I was delighted to be going to my place, but at the same time I was remembering all the times I arrived home and Aunt Josephine would be waiting for me to return. Then what came to mind was the time Aunt Josephine wasn't at home

19

when I arrived. I felt very disappointed when I walked into an empty house. She had left me a note explaining that she had gone to a floristry exhibition in Belgium and wouldn't be back until Saturday. Would I have the same feeling when I arrived at my place and nobody was home? I remembered how without Aunt Josephine at home I felt like I was hanging about. I really didn't like being at home without her. After a day or two, I had done all my washing, cleared my room and changed the bedding. I decided to go and stay over at May's place. Our family home never seemed comfortable when there wasn't anyone else at home. May and I had a nice couple of days and did lots of chatting. I had told her my plan to buy my own house and settle down with someone special, hopefully.

I finally arrived back at my place, for the first time since I moved in. As I opened the door, the place was so still – not a sound, nothing. Paul and Sophie had been staying, yes, but there wasn't a trace that they had ever been there. While it was nice that they had tidied up after themselves, the lack of any sign of them made me feel lonely. I remember thinking to myself, 'Surely they must have left something untidy', but there wasn't anything – I looked everywhere – not even a sweet wrapper. This was my place and my place alone. This was going to take some getting used to. Paul and Sophie had left the place spotless. I started to feel slightly sorry for myself.

I walked over to the shop and bought some milk and bread. While in the shop I realised I needed to do my washing, so when I got back I made a cup of tea, sat down and ordered a washing machine and dryer to be delivered within the next couple of days I also need a dining table and chairs, but that could wait until one of my sisters could help choose, as well as curtains, and blinds. Up till then, I had not realised just how much stuff I needed to make a house a home. I had a month's leave, so I decided that I was going to make sure I bought everything I needed this time before I went back on duty.

That weekend May and Vy came over and we went furniture shopping. May had measured up the windows for curtains and Vy had arranged for the local blind shop to visit to measure up the windows and make the blinds. The fellow from the blind shop had brought his assistant along and this lady could make curtains, so May decided to let them make the curtains as well as the blinds. The pair were very good and knew their job. They picked out some very nice fabrics, and my sisters were very happy. It was going to take six weeks to make them because of the Christmas holidays, by which time I would be back on duty. But the girls kindly offered to make the arrangements to meet them back at my place so they could fit the blinds and put the curtains up, and I knew the girls would make sure everything was in order. I had arranged to take the girls and Aunt Josephine out for dinner that evening, so after we'd finished sorting out my windows, we picked up Aunt Josephine. She had warned us that she had something she wanted to tell us all, and for some reason I thought she was going to tell us that she wanted to sell the flower shop. We all arrived at the restaurant and once we'd settled in and ordered our food Aunt Josephine told us that she had met someone else, that she had been going out with him for some time, and that she thought it best that we all meet him. The girls looked very surprised. Aunt Josephine explained that she had already told Khan and Jon and that they were happy for her. I could see that she was nervous telling me and the girls. There was an awkward silence, but only for a matter of seconds before the girls realised. They both stood up and hugged their mother, and both girls told her that they were surprised but at the same time very happy for her.

Aunt Josephine looked at me and said, 'How do you feel about this, Sean?'

I smiled and said, 'I'm very pleased to hear this, and as long as you are happy then we are happy for you.'

Aunt Josephine told us, 'I would very much like you all to meet Alex, so he has arranged dinner at his place for all of us – including the grandchildren – next Friday. I do hope you can all be there?'

We all replied that yes, of course we would be there, and a look of relief appeared on Aunt Josephine's face. The very hardest part – breaking the news – was done, and we could get back to being a family again.

'But are we all going to fit into Alex's place for dinner?' I asked.

Aunt Josephine started to get a bit embarrassed – I could see she was blushing.

Vy said, 'Mother, you've gone red.'

'Yes,' she replied. 'Well, you see, Alex has got a big place. Too big, actually. He lives in a stately home, with fifteen bedrooms.'

We all started to laugh because by the time she'd finished speaking, Aunt Josephine was completely red-faced.

'Oh, Mother, please. If Alex owns a stately home, that's nothing to be embarrassed about.'

'Yes, yes, I know. But you know how I feel talking about things that don't belong to us. I didn't know he had a stately home until about three months into the relationship.'

Vy said jokingly, 'I bet you wouldn't have gone out with him if you'd known that before.'

Aunt Josephine, as quick lighting, said, 'No. No, of course not.' Then she paused, realising what she had said, and started to laugh. 'I'm being ridiculous,' she added before going quiet.

'So how long have you been going out with Alex?' I asked.

'Six months next week.'

We all held hands around the table.

'Mother,' Vy said, 'we are all very happy for you, and you deserve to be happy.'

May continued, 'Yes, we all know that you sacrificed your younger life for us.'

I told Josephine, 'May's right. If anybody deserves happiness, it's you.'

Josephine smiled proudly and replied, 'So you all will be able to make next Friday?'

'Yes,' we all said together.

May asked, 'How did you meet Alex? You're never out of the shop!'

'Well,' Josephine looked at May, 'it's your fault really! Remember that Saturday when you felt unwell and we were doing the flowers for that big wedding at the big stately home?'

May replied, 'Of course. I'll never forget that. We visited the venue twice because the mother of the bride was so fussy. She changed the colour of the flowers, then she wasn't sure so we made up a sample garland and took it to the venue.'

'That's correct,' said Josephine. 'And then what happened on the day of the wedding, May?'

May thought for a moment and then replied, 'Do you know, I can't remember.'

Josephine nodded and smiled. 'No, because you took ill the night before.'

'That's right,' said May. 'I never did see the finished product.'

'Well,' Josephine went on, 'I had forgotten that Jean had booked that Saturday off also.'

May replied, 'You're joking. You never said. How did you manage?'

'You should have phoned me,' Vy said.

'It was far too late for all that. I just got on with the job. I allowed myself an extra hour, which I used up at the church. Then when I arrived at the reception venue—'

'Don't tell me that Alex owns the wedding venue!' May blurted out.

Josephine blushed again like a teenager. She somehow had a youthful look about her, and I knew at this point I was going to like Alex.

Josephine said, 'Yes, May. Now, are you going to let me finish?'

'Yes! Go on!' we all said at the same time. We were all feeling very excited.

Josephine carried on. 'Well, no May, no Jean. I got the church finished, then I rushed back to the shop to pick up all the table arrangements and the garlands, and then I made my way over to the house. As I started to unload the van, a fellow walked over and said to me, "You're cutting it fine." And without thinking, I asked him if he could help me. He never hesitated and replied, "Yes, of course." As I looked around I could just see the bride and her father leaving for the church, so I only had roughly one hour and thirty minutes or so. We got everything indoors and I started to dress the tables. The fellow watched, and then he started dressing them himself. He was very good, and quick, so I presumed he must have been the groundsman.'

Josephine went on. 'We got it all done just before the bridal party arrived back at the house. I was sweating, especially knowing the mother of the bride was so picky. After we'd finished, the fellow said, "I think it's time for a cup of tea." I was so grateful to him that I dared not refuse, even though I wanted to get back to the shop because it was Saturday I would be missing out on trade. He held out his hand and said, "I'm Alex." I shook his hand and said, "Nice to meet you. I'm Josephine." Then he said, "Follow me, and we will go through to the kitchen." I never thought anything other than it would be the quickest cup of tea ever. We made small talk over our cup of tea, then I thanked him very much for his help. Then, just before I left, he told me I owed him a drink. I smiled and, not thinking too much about it, I replied, "You're on." I left the house feeling very grateful to Alex.'

We listened intently as Josephine continued her story. 'The following Saturday, Alex came into the shop. There was just me and Jean this Saturday. He looked very smart and very handsome, and quite different from the Alex from the big house that I had met the previous Saturday. He was wearing a pale blue shirt and matching tie, navy blue trousers, a black leather belt and a beautiful pair of navy blue loafers, so shiny you could see your reflection in them. I didn't even recognise him to start with. It was only when he spoke that I remembered who he was.'

May said, 'I can't believe this! All the time I've spent in that shop, then I'm away for two Saturdays and all this happens.'

Josephine said with a polite smile are you going to let me finish?

25

By that point, we were all so excited that it was hard to think about eating our dinner.

Josephine carried on. 'He said, "Hello, Josephine. I've come to get that drink you owe me." I was very surprised to see him, I have to be honest. I replied, "It's Saturday, and there is only me and Jean here too, so I cannot possibly leave the shop today." Alex looked around and spotted Jean, then he walked towards her and said, "Hello, Jean. I'm Alex." Jean quickly replied, "Nice to meet you." Alex went on: "Did you enjoy your Saturday away last week?" By this time both Jean and I are bright red and giggling like teenagers; we both felt so silly. Jean replied, "Yes, it was lovely, thank you. Why do you ask?" Alex replied, "Because while you were away this good lady, Josephine, got me to do your job." Jean said, "I'm really sorry, but I did book in advance." Alex said, "Don't be sorry – it was one of the best morning's work I've ever done. However," Alex carried on he looked round at me and said to Jean, "Josephine has promised to buy me a drink, and a promise is a promise. So, Jean, would it be the end of the world if I took Josephine out of the shop today so I can get my drink? In all fairness, you do owe me a drink, Josephine," he said with a grin. Jean quickly replied, "I will be fine in here today. We don't even have any deliveries to make." I looked at Alex. I was still bright red like a teenager and feeling sick and hungry at the same time. I never imagined I would ever feel like that again, but I did, and to be totally honest – and I hope won't mind me saying this – I felt so excited I almost cried.'

We all looked at Aunt Josephine and started to laugh with joy. We all felt more than happy for her. If anybody deserved happiness it was Josephine. She was a good, honest, strong woman who had devoted her life to her children in every way possible. She had never left our side, not for one minute. Wherever she went, we all went with her – holidays, theatre, cinema, swimming, shopping, out for dinner, out to lunch. Whatever Josephine did, we did as a family. We were united.

May said, 'This is magic, Mother. The stuff you only hear about in fairy tales. This is so exciting. I cannot wait to meet him.'

I asked Aunt Josephine, 'Did you leave the shop?'

The girls started to laugh.

Josephine sighed and said, 'After about ten minutes I decided it was very nice of Alex, and it would be very rude of me not to buy him a drink, as he put it. I think it was the only time I was really glad the shop was next to the house, and I told Alex, "If I'm going to buy you a drink, I would need to have a quick wash and change." Still feeling like a teenager, I quickly washed and changed. I was so quick that I felt like Wonderwoman!'

May asked, 'Where did you go?'

'We went to that lovely hotel – I cannot remember the name. It's on the way to Caldicot, and it's got its own golf course, do you know?'

Vy said, 'Yes, I know, it's the De Vere brand.'

'That's it,' Josephine said. 'Looking back now, I've never asked, but I think he must have booked that straight after I left the house, the morning of the wedding because I've tried a couple of times and I can never get in there. It's always fully booked.'

'Wow, this just gets better,' I said. 'When is the wedding?' I added cheekily.

Excitement turned to laughter again.

'Now, don't be silly, Sean. It would take a hell of a lot for an old gal like me to get married again.'

27

With that, my father popped into my head. In fact, as I picked up my head and looked around the table, it seemed as if he'd popped into everyone's head, and the conversation had come to a standstill.

I needed to think of something quick. 'You would never be lucky enough to find another like our father,' I quipped.

Josephine smiled and replied, 'Let's hope not.'

Vy quickly followed up with 'So, how did you get on?'

'Very well. We had a lovely day.'

May asked, 'When did you realise that Alex wasn't the groundsman but the owner of the house?'

Josephine replied, 'It was about three months into the relationship. Alex asked me to visit his house because he wanted to cook for me. I agreed, not thinking too much about it. Then he said, "Would you like me to pick you up?" I refused and said, "No, I can bring myself to your place, surely." He replied, "Yes, I'm sure you will find us." I thought for a moment and wondered why Alex would suggest for him to come pick me up – perhaps his place was very awkward to get to, or maybe it's not in a nice area? Then a stupid childish thought entered my head – what about if Alex's place is in the deep, dark woods? I was in deep thought and in a world of my own, so Alex asked me if I was okay. I replied, "Yes, I'm just thinking about the deliveries tomorrow." I remember thinking to myself that he would think I was silly if I told him what was really on my mind. Then I decided that I'd better ask just whereabouts Alex's place is so that I can plan my route, just in case it is awkward to find. That way, not only I will be able to see for myself, but I could even do a practice run. This was a big thing for me. I've had my independence for many years, and I didn't need Alex to pick me up. The whole idea sounded stupid. However, I was still wondering why Alex would have suggested picking me up. "So tell me, Alex, where do you live?" I asked him. I could see an anxious look come over his face, which made us both feel uncomfortable. It felt like I shouldn't ask that question. And that's when I found out that Alex was the owner of the stately house that I had decorated for the wedding. Alex was the owner of the wedding venue. Alex wasn't the groundsman – he was the owner. I then realised that Alex was a modest man, and I had the feeling that his home seemed to be a burden to him. Then I felt slightly out of my depth. Alex still had that anxious look on his face, so I smiled and said, "On second thoughts, I think it's best for you to pick me up." With that, a look of relief came over his face and he said, "I don't want you to feel intimidated by my home. Like most people, I love my home. However, my home isn't just my home. It has to be my place of work too, for me to be able to live there. The upkeep on a property of that size and that age is staggering." I told Alex that I understood what he was saying. "That's why you rent out the rooms for weddings etc," I said. Alex replied, "Exactly. We have to work the property to its maximum potential to be able to keep up the maintenance and daily expenses of running and owning it."'

Josephine sipped her water while we all waited for more. 'After that conversation, I got the feeling that Alex's home was not only a burden but also very hard work. I asked him if he had ever considered downsizing. "It's out of the question," he said. "The house has been in our family for generations, and I'm not going to be the generation that fails." So that gave me a clear picture of why his home is a burden. Alex told me that the very thought of failure gave him the drive to keep the house going.'

I was reminded of just how sensible Aunt Josephine was. Such a wise woman who seemed to know all the answers – not in a self-righteous way, but more like she understands the answers. It's hard to explain, but Josephine seems to be able to grasp all walks of life and always keeps both feet on the ground.

Vy asked, 'Has Alex got any children?'

'Yes. He has two daughters – Maria and Shannon – and one son, Tom.'

I asked, 'Have you met them?'

'I've only met Maria and Tom. Shannon lives in Los Angeles. Shannon married an American. He's an accountant and he's got a job working for a big company. Apparently, it's a really well-paid job. Maria's the youngest and she's not married, and Tom lives and works on the estate with his wife Teigen and two children – Alexander, who's nine, and Marcus, who's seven.'

May asked, 'Will they be at Alex's house next Friday?'

'Yes. All of Alex's family will be there, except Shannon, so Alex has asked Shannon to do face time.'

I started to wonder about Alex's wife. Josephine must have read my mind. 'Alex was happily married for thirty-two years. However, his wife was a career woman and she had a high-flying job that would take her away for days at a time, and over time they grew apart. I don't think anybody else was involved. She just loved her job, and Alex loved his estate, and there wasn't room for compromise.'

'What's her name?' I asked.

'Lisa.'

'Where does Lisa live now?'

'Just outside London. Not too far from Heathrow Airport, in a little place called Datchet.

'Well, I have to say, Aunt Josephine, this all sounds very interesting, and I'm looking forward to meeting everybody next Friday,' I said.

Josephine smiled and said, 'You will like Alex, Sean. He is a kind man. He had a very good education so is very knowledgeable and hard-working. And, like me, he believes family is everything. The estate is his main job as it's very large. There are two farms, which are rented out. The dairy farm is the smaller of the two, and the larger one is crops and cattle. Then Alex and Tom manage the house and its grounds. They both work very hard because the house is a large eighteenth-century mansion, so it constantly needs attention, and attention costs money – in their case a lot of money. So it's all very hard work.'

Vy asked, 'What about Maria? What's her part in all this?'

'By the sound of things, she doesn't do a great deal when it comes to the estate. She has a job in town as a reporter and editor for the local paper. Alex said she likes being out and about, getting to know people, finding out their stories and making news of it. She is good at her job but doesn't really make much money. That's why she lives on the estate – because she cannot afford a place of her own. Alex said she pays her way by helping out one day a week with paperwork for the estate. I suppose Maria is a happy-go-lucky person.'

Our evening meal was coming to an end. We reassured Josephine that we would all definitely be there next Friday. After coffee, I picked up the bill and it was time to leave. We dropped off Aunt Josephine first, then May dropped me home, back to my place. How I loved saying 'my place'. The girls stayed for a while and I made a cup of tea for us all. We chatted about Aunt Josephine and Alex, and then about what had been happening while I'd been away from usual family stuff.

*

The next day was Saturday and I was going out for the day with Khan and Jon. Khan had arranged for us to visit a vintage classics car show in the morning, and then in the afternoon we were all meeting for lunch at Khan's favourite pub just outside Chepstow. It's a big place with a nice garden and playground for the kids, so it's ideal for us. The next day, bang on 7.30 am, Khan and Jon were knocking on my door. I was doing the breakfast that morning for us three – bacon, eggs and all the trimmings. It was great – I'm not a bad cook, to be honest. After breakfast, we all quickly cleaned up the kitchen and washed up the pots. One more cup of tea and then we left, as planned, at 8.15 am.

The classic car show was taking place in Cardiff, and we arrived there just after 9 am. There were some beautiful old cars; it's not really my thing, but it's a good excuse to spend time with my brothers, and we always manage to laugh, plus you never know what you might see. We weren't there that long – we left around 11.30 am and headed to the pub.

The plan was for the girls to pick up Aunt Josephine. Linda and the children were making their own way there, so hopefully, by the time we arrived, everybody would be there. Khan likes to organise us, you see. Khan is married to Linda and they have two little girls: Indiana is seven and Nevada is five. Jon has a girlfriend, Fay, who he has been living with for the last five years – they do plan to get married someday. They are both very ambitious, so work always stands in the way when it comes to future plans, but they both seem very happy together. Khan is and always has been a family guy; everything with Khan is family. He is a devoted father, husband, son and brother.

Vy is now working as a legal secretary for a group of barristers. She hopes to be a prosecution barrister one day. Vy hasn't got a partner as of yet – she's had a few boyfriends in the past but nothing serious because she enjoys her work too much. Vy told me that practising law takes up a lot of time. Everything is based on reputation, so to maintain a good reputation you must leave no stone unturned. When a barrister starts putting a defence case together it's like cleaning out the loft that's been left for twenty years – one speck of dust can be the difference between winning and losing the case, so making sure the loft is spotless is very important.

May mostly helps Aunt Josephine with the shop and two days a week in the charity shop. I believe that once Josephine retires, May will buy the flower shop. May has got a boyfriend – if you can call him that, and I have my doubts about that. Thankfully, Jeff was not joining us for dinner.

As we arrived at the pub at 12.45. It's a nice pub with a good atmosphere, and the landlord knows everyone, so it feels like a home from home. We had a great afternoon, and a lot of the conversation was about Alex; everybody had a question they wanted to ask in readiness for next Friday. Aunt Josephine seemed very happy and loved answering all the questions. Everything about Alex seemed positive and sensible. It almost felt too good to be true.

I noticed a big difference in Josephine. She looked and sounded happier. It felt like she had somehow become one of us. She had slipped out of being the role model for the time being. It was her time now. We all felt the difference, and we were happy for her.

As I looked around the room at all my family, a thought entered my head: I hoped Alex would be as good as Aunt Josephine wanted him to be, because if not, this would have an impact on us all. Aunt Josephine was everything to us: our mother and father at the same time, our guide and strength, the light at the end of the tunnel, our umbrella on a wet day. If Alex were to let Josephine down, he would be letting us all down.

I asked Aunt Josephine, 'Has Alex asked about us?'

She replied, 'Yes, many times, and I've told him how proud of you all I am.'

I loved her answer – ever the wise woman. I felt relieved. After a nice afternoon, we all left the pub around 6 pm and headed home.

Chapter Three

∽

My week ahead was pretty straightforward. Josephine asked me to help with a few jobs around her house on the Monday – she was taking the day off, so I spent it with her. There were only a few little jobs to do, so I think it was just an excuse so she could make us a lovely dinner. I love being with Aunt Josephine – it reminds me of how lucky I've been in life.

The next day my washing machine and dryer arrived. Fitting them was easy, using what plumbing skills I already had, and I decided that when I left the military that would be my job. Jon had already told me that there is a shortage of plumbers, and you can earn up to 80K a year. If I bought a van I could go self-employed and then I could work my own hours. I would probably need to look into courses so that I could get the qualifications needed.

I thought about doing the Christmas shopping. For some reason, I didn't feel good about going, but I couldn't put my finger on what was causing me to feel anxious. Still, with Christmas only four weeks away I decided that I would need to get on with it that week. I wanted to shop local this year, and maybe that was what was causing me to feel anxious. At that time of year, subconsciously I was probably thinking about my natural mum – plus there would be the possibility of running into my father. I decided to put my thoughts to the back of my mind, as I always do, and focus. They weren't my family. And if I did come across them, what difference would it make? None.

I was only hurting myself by thinking about my natural parents. The festive season approaching didn't make any difference to the situation. It's such a shame that I put myself through this, but I suppose it's because I'm a nice person, and no child of mine will ever be left for someone else to pick up. Even though I had a perfectly good upbringing I would always wonder: Would my life have been any better? Would I have been a different person? In all honesty, what I was putting myself through wasn't fair to my family. I settled myself down, knowing that I'm the person I am today because of Aunt Josephine, my brothers and sisters. And, because of the amazing family I have, I know that I would never, ever leave my children. My natural parents are not worth thinking about. Christmas sometimes can be a difficult time of the year, and any other time these people wouldn't enter my head. The problem is, I suppose, that the world paints such a perfect picture of Christmas, and the reality is that it's just another day. Why did I put myself through these miserable ideas? I was old enough to know better and wise enough to move on. After all those negative thoughts, I reminded myself that Khan's children would be getting very excited now that Christmas was almost here, and I hoped I would find them something really special to buy them for Christmas.

I would normally travel to Bristol or Cardiff for shopping; however, I felt that wasn't necessary anymore as we had a perfectly beautiful little town with some very nice shops. I made my way into town and after visiting a few shops I had bought almost everyone something nice for Christmas. I needed a break by then, so I spotted a nice coffee shop and decided to stop there. I picked up the local paper, ordered my coffee and found a table by the window. Just across the road from the coffee shop was an army and navy surplus store – I hadn't noticed this before. While I drank my coffee I was pondering what I was going to get Indiana and Nevada for Christmas, and when I looked at the surplus store, it came to me. I would ask Khan if I could make them a military-style den in the back garden because I knew they liked playing outdoors. It was perfect because I was spending the coming weekend alone, and for some reason, I wasn't looking forward to it. I could ask Khan if I could make the den over the weekend while Khan's family were visiting Linda's parents.

I was sitting in the coffee shop feeling very proud of myself for having come up with such a good idea. I phoned Khan to make sure my idea was okay with him and Linda. Like me, Khan thought the idea was great, and he wanted it to be a surprise for the children in the same way I did, so he was going to find a way to partition the bottom end of the garden so that the children wouldn't realise what was going on. Between us, we worked out exactly how to get the den built without the children knowing what we were up to. Khan also had a very nice garage full of tools that I could use, and he was going to drop off the spare house keys at my place on Friday, before we all met up at Alex's place with Aunt Josephine.

I finished my coffee and walked across to the army and navy surplus store. They had everything I needed: the camouflage canvas, waterproof covers, and camouflage netting. I decided to focus on the military because that represented me – it would also have more of an outdoor theme. After the surplus store, I walked over to the charity shop and bought some blankets. I also picked up some children's books and old records, which I planned to hang up for decoration. And then I picked up some old CDs, found an old battery radio and some old trophies. The charity shop felt like a little treasure trove, and my imagination was running wild. It felt like I could create a place of inspiration. All the little things I had picked up were going to make for good decorations.

Then I went to a camping shop and bought battery-powered lighting. I felt myself really enjoying my idea, and I picked up a solar panel, which powered a small light. Indiana and Nevada were going to love my idea – I was sure of it. The final thing I needed was some wood, so I ordered that to be delivered straight to Khan's house.

Shopping done, I decided I would have dinner out. I made my way over to the Coach Inn – a lovely friendly place with good food. When I walked in, I felt at home straight away. It's a real old English pub – a low ceiling with solid oak beams running right through, with solid oak supports, and real wooden floorboards that creaked as soon as you walked in. The bar is beautiful, made from old English oak, and it catches your eye as soon as you walk in, and seems to tell you that you're in for a good time. If there is one thing we know how to do properly in the UK it's pubs – nothing can beat a proper pint in a proper English pub, and you can always be sure of a good steak and ale pie – a real treat with a nice pint.

While I was enjoying my dinner I noticed a couple of my muckers from the barracks walk in, so after dinner a couple more drinks were in order as we were having a nice time and it was good to see them in a social capacity. We had lots to talk about – and without realising it we had lots to drink too. As time went on, a few more of our lads joined us and we became very loud without realising. The landlord came over and asked us to try and be a bit quieter, and I felt the atmosphere change slightly. I decided not to drink any more because I noticed that the locals weren't pleased with us. I asked the boys to calm down but they were too far gone by then, and I could see this wasn't going to end well.

I phoned Jon and asked if he was able to pick me up. I told him not to park by the pub, to park further up the road and I would walk to him.

'Just phone me when you arrive,' I told him.

Jon must have sensed something wasn't right because just before I put the phone down he said, 'I'm coming straight away.'

I wasn't going to tell the lads I was leaving – I was just going to slip away.

But before Jon got to me, it kicked off: one of the lads had been chatting to a young lady, and the guy she was with didn't like it and thought the lad was being far too friendly. Personally, I wasn't so sure about his take on things – I think *she* was being far too friendly. It turned into an all-out war in this beautiful little pub – I could see the landlord he had a look of despair on his face, and this saddened me. I tried to stop the fighting but the lads were too drunk. The fighting seemed to go on for ages, and by the time it was finished, the pub was in a terrible mess. The police arrived, made sure nobody was seriously hurt and left once they realised most of us were from the barracks. The landlord was furious; his wife was crying. I felt so sorry for them, and embarrassed that my muckers – trained soldiers who I know have worked very hard and gained the utmost respect – had turned the beautiful little pub on its head over nothing, and the police had just let them get away with it without so much has a slap on the wrist. I suppose, looking back, I don't blame them. It was one big mess, and nobody was seriously hurt.

At that point Jon phoned me, and I told him I was coming. My muckers were all outside by then, but I didn't say a word, just walked away. They were all starting to see just what they had done by then. On the way home, Jon asked what had happened so I told him. Jon never said much; he was just glad I was okay. I asked him not to mention this to the girls or Aunt Josephine.

The next morning I felt awful. I couldn't get out of bed, even though I'd stopped drinking quite early because I'm not really a drinker. The hangover was terrible, and the famous last words – 'never again' – came to mind. I realised I had left all my Christmas shopping back at the pub, so once I felt okay I would need to go back to the pub, and I was dreading walking back in there. I got myself up; I couldn't eat anything, so I just had a cup of coffee. I straightened myself up and made my way back over to the pub. When I arrived it looked much worse than it did the night before. I felt so embarrassed, even though I'd tried very hard to defuse the situation. This mess was the result of my muckers. The landlord must have been out the back because there was no one in sight, so I decided to start tidying up, because I felt like I needed to do something, and I found a sweeping brush and made a start. About half an hour must have passed before the landlord's wife walked in. She looked shocked and asked me what I was doing.

I felt so guilty. 'I was here last night,' I told her.

She looked at me again and said, 'Yes, I remember you. I suppose you've come to collect your Christmas shopping?'

I replied, 'Yes, that was my first thought for coming here this morning, but when I walked and saw all this mess

I felt very embarrassed, and I know my muckers would feel the same, so I started to tidy up.'

'Yes, I can see what you are doing,' she said in a stern voice.

I carried on, and she just sat there in a world of her own. After a while, the landlord was still nowhere to be seen, so I asked if the landlord was okay.

She shook her head. 'No. After we finally got everybody out last night, Mike had a heart attack,'

This was getting worse. She started to cry, and I felt sick with guilt and anger.

'I'm so sorry,' I said.

'Yes, so am I. I'm sorry that we ever took this pub on.' Then she stood up, adding, 'I'm not opening today. I've told my staff not to come in. Your shopping is where you left it.'

'Okay,' I replied, 'but I'm not leaving until this pub it's ready to open again.'

She looked at me and said, 'Good luck with that, because I'm going to get some sleep before I have a heart attack myself.'

'Will Mike be okay?' I plucked up the courage to ask.

'He will be. He just needs plenty of rest. But with Christmas on the horizon, I'm not sure how Mike is supposed to rest.'

Without thinking, I said, 'I'm on leave. I would be more than happy to help you as much as I can over the festive season.'

She looked very surprised, and with her stern tone of voice said, 'Why would you do that?'

I thought for a moment and replied, 'Because, as I said, I'm on leave, and I don't like what happened here last night. My muckers were wrong. They should have just

41

walked out. And I'm sure they will be feeling very bad today, as I do.'

I could see she wasn't really listening to me – and who could blame her after the night she'd had? She went upstairs, leaving me to clean up.

After about six hours the pub was somewhere near back to normal. At that point, a young, very attractive woman walked in. She had a medium build, about five foot six tall, with dark brown hair and shining blue eyes. As I looked at her I felt the room spinning – only this time it wasn't because of the drink I had consumed the night before, instead it was her beautiful eyes and olive skin – she had a Mediterranean look about her. I felt very intrigued by this woman, but I tore my eyes away and carried on cleaning up, trying to go unnoticed.

But she walked over to me and asked, 'Is Jo around?'

She had a soft tone of voice, which I loved.

'Is Jo the landlady?' I asked.

'Yes. Who are you?'

'I'm Sean.'

'May I ask what are you doing, Sean?'

'I'm cleaning up.'

'After last night? Were *you* here last night?'

Too many questions, I thought to myself. Time to ask a few myself. 'Please may I ask who you are? And why are you asking me so many questions?'

She smiled at me very nicely as if to say, oops, you got me. 'Sorry, sorry, yes, of course. Let me introduce myself. I'm a reporter, and my name is Maria.'

The penny dropped – she was *that* Maria, Alex's daughter. I smiled back very nicely, and Maria went bright red. A thought shot into my head: should I tell her exactly who I am? Then the answer came even quicker: NO. There may well be another reporter called Maria, and that would make me look silly.

'Question one,' I said, 'yes, I was here last night, and I'm very sorry but I cannot talk to any reporters about last night because it's not my place to do so. Question two, Jo is upstairs.'

Maria looked at me and said, 'A wise response. I will wait for Jo to come down.'

I carried on cleaning up.

'Do you want me to help while I'm waiting?' Maria asked me.

'I've almost done everything that I can do for now, but thanks,' I replied.

Jo emerged then – she must have heard us talking. She looked around, looked at me, and said, 'Wow, fair play, you've done an excellent job, young man. I'm sorry about earlier – I was just so tired.'

I replied, 'Not to worry – I'm just glad I could do something to help. But if you're okay I'm going to pick up my shopping and get out of your way.'

Joe nodded. 'Yes, I'll be fine. My staff are coming in first thing tomorrow morning. I'm going back to the hospital now to visit Mike – but tell me, young man, what is your name?'

'I'm Sean.'

'I'm Jo.' She held out her hand.

I shook it. 'Yes, I already know your name. Maria, the reporter, is waiting to see you.'

'Oh – okay,' she replied, then she whispered, 'I don't want any reports about what happened here last night. You haven't said anything, have you?'

'No. Definitely not.'

'Good. I will work this to my advantage.' I had no idea what she meant by that.

43

'I meant what I said earlier,' I told her. 'I can help you if you need.'

'You know what – that would be helpful, because Mike is a key part of running this pub, and he is going to need plenty of rest.'

'Okay, no problem. Like I said, I'm on leave.'

I then quickly spotted an opportunity to see if Maria was indeed *that* Maria. I waited for Jo to walk over to Maria, then I walked over to where both women were sitting and said, 'Sorry to interrupt, but I thought I'd better let you know I can't help on Friday, as I've got to be somewhere else.'

Maria quickly turned her head and looked straight at me. It was something I'll never forget; we looked at each other and both smiled at the same time. Some memories are pure treasures.

'Can you come in tomorrow to help me get started back up?' Jo asked, oblivious to the connection being made in the room.

'Yes, of course. What time?'

'10 am?'

'Yes, that's fine. See you tomorrow, and I hope Mike will be okay.'

I could see Jo's massive relief when I told her that I will be back the next day.

I looked one more time at Maria. 'See you Friday,' I grinned.

She smiled back very brightly, and I felt butterflies – a feeling I had not experienced in a long time.

I was smiling to myself all the way home.

*

Once I got home I unpacked my shopping. I was really pleased with myself as I had managed to get everyone something nice. We don't spend a great deal of money on presents in our family; it's more about the gesture than the gift. When we were all children Aunt Josephine would make sure that we only asked Santa for one present, and then she would buy a few surprises – but she never went over the top. Aunt Josephine's main focus at Christmas time was Christmas dinner and being together – that was the most important thing to her, and she was right. We had a very nice Christmas – it was special.

I started to think about how I was going to put the den together. I drew it out so I could imagine better how it would look. I felt like a child again because I was so excited and I know Indiana and Nevada were going to love it.

The next day I returned to the pub at 10 am, as Jo had asked me to. On the way, I couldn't help but think of Maria. Just the thought of her perfect smile made me grin. Her eyes were deep blue and I couldn't stop myself from thinking about them, though I suppressed my thoughts as best as I could. Maria may well have a boyfriend – that thought alone made me feel disappointed. Then I questioned myself – why did I feel like this? I didn't even know Maria, she had just made an impression on me, and I should just leave it there. Still, I couldn't. I wondered if Maria would be visiting the pub that day.

When I arrived I noticed the cellar doors were open and cordoned off. I walked into the pub, where I saw Jo was very busy putting all the deliveries in place.

Jo saw me and said, 'Thank you for coming in today.'

'No problem. What would you like me to do?'

'The brewery will be delivering within the next thirty minutes. Can you take the delivery and make sure it's correct?'

'Yes, of course,' I replied, not really understanding what exactly it entailed. Jo gave me the order sheet and pointed me to the cellar, which was accessed via what Jo called the stock room. The cellar door was half the size of a standard door, and the staircase which led down was also half the size of a standard staircase. There was no doubt that this was a job for a smaller person than me – I'm six foot two. I discovered that the cellar was also very cramped, but I didn't take any notice because there was a nice breeze passing through the open door. I walked over and looked up – there was a rope, and I soon realised that the barrels would need to be lowered down into the cellar. Once I'd familiarised myself with the cellar I decided it would be best for me to wait outside, just in case anybody risked falling down into the cellar; even though it was cordoned off, you can never be too safe. The cellar felt damp and cold and the floor was wet with a few little puddles. I looked down at my feet because they felt wet – my shoes were not right for this job, but there wasn't anything I could do now except get on with the job in hand and put up with the wet feet for today.

After a few minutes, the brewery truck arrived. 'Where's Mike today?' the driver asked as he got out of the truck.

I felt sick. Not wanting to say too much, I replied, 'He's unwell today.'

'He must be dying,' the driver quipped. 'I've seen him very unwell and he still manages to run this place.' Then the driver stopped and thought about what he had just said. 'Seriously, is Mike okay?'

I opened my mouth but stopped. 'Listen, I've never done this before, so let's just get the job done, and you can go a speak to Jo yourself.'

I could see the driver was genuinely concerned, and he replied, 'Yes, yes, of course. My name's Ken, by the way. What's yours?'

I held out my hand and said, 'I'm Sean.'

Ken got straight on with the job, showing me the ropes – literally. I could see Ken wasn't a very nice guy. One by one, we lowered all ten barrels into the cellar using the rope. Once I got the hang of it, it was easy, and in no time we were done. Ken showed me how to close the cellar doors and then he went inside to see Jo. I took down the cordon – I assumed it was stored in the cellar. When I walked back into the pub I noticed Ken and Jo deep in conversation. Jo still looked very worried, and Ken was clearly shocked by what Jo was telling him. This was all a very sad affair. I noticed that the chef had just arrived. He didn't speak to anyone, just went straight into the kitchen. There was also a young lad laying the tables and a woman who looked the same age as Jo getting the bar ready. Everybody there seemed to know their job and was well organised about doing it. I wondered what my next job would be.

I could see Jo and Ken were still deep in conversation, so I walked over to the lady behind the bar. 'Hello, I'm Sean.'

'Hello, I'm Judith – Jo's big sister.'

'Do you need me to do anything?'

'Yes. Can you re-stock the drinks cooler, please? You'll find all the stock in the stock room.' I looked at the cooler to see what was needed, and then went to find all of it and got everything that was needed for the cooler. With that done, I looked around and noticed Jo was still in deep conversation with Ken. I went outside to check if his lorry was still there, and it was. It wasn't parked in anybody's way, so I supposed Ken could stay for dinner. I was looking around to see if I could find myself something else to do – if there's one thing I cannot put up with, it's hanging about. Jo could see I was getting bored, so she asked me if I would go out the back and sweep the beer garden.

I was glad to get out of the pub – Jo and Ken were getting on my nerves. As I swept, I started to wonder if Mike was going to be okay. Then I hoped nobody else was waiting for a brewery delivery, because old Friar Tuck was otherwise engaged. To be honest, Ken and Jo looked very suspicious, standing very close together while they talked – no wonder poor old Mike had a heart attack if that was how Jo carried on. I decided to take my time sweeping out the beer garden in the hope that Ken would be gone by the time I'd finished. Perhaps I was overthinking this though; Ken could be a relation – a first cousin maybe.

After an hour there wasn't anything left to sweep so, like it or not, I needed to go back into the pub. Just as I walked in, Jo and Friar Tuck were heading upstairs. I felt sick. Poor old Mike was in the hospital, having just had a heart attack, and old Friar Tuck is about to have a fuck with his wife. I looked at Judith, and I could see she was so angry. I didn't say anything and nor did she.

After a long, uncomfortable silence, I said, 'Does old Friar Tuck come here often?'

She looked at me and burst out laughing. When she'd composed herself again she said, 'Please forgive me for laughing. It's not right – dear Mike laid up in the hospital, and she was up there with Ken.' I could see Judith was genuinely angry with her sister.

I didn't say anything else; my suspicious mind was correct. I just wanted to get out of there. I walked into the kitchen to see if the chef needed any help, and I could see he wasn't very happy either.

'Hello, I'm Sean.'

'Hello, Sean. I'm Carlos.'

'I've just come to see if you need any help.'

'No, I can manage, thank you. Wednesday is a quiet day.' I turned to leave, but then Carlos asked me, in an angry tone of voice, 'Is Ken still here?'

I was lost for words, so I just shrugged my shoulders. I wasn't going to chance my Friar Tuck line again.

It turned out that Carlos was angrier than Judith. 'Mike's such a nice guy. She doesn't deserve him.'

I got the feeling that old Friar Tuck called in regularly. Now I really wanted to leave – this wasn't for me. I'd been brought up with a good moral code. I didn't even know Jo, and now I was feeling dislike towards her.

Then Carlos said, out of the blue, 'She was fucking Mike's best friend until Mike found out.'

I really started to feel sorry for Mike,

'It'll be you upstairs next,' Carlos quipped.

I looked very sternly at Carlos and replied, 'No thank you.'

As I walked out from the kitchen, Ken was just coming down the stairs and at the same time he was fastening up his belt with a smug look on his face, Jo was behind, doing up her top. I had never felt so uncomfortable. I waited for Friar Tuck to get back into his truck and leave, and then I told Jo that I was leaving.

She was shocked. 'But I thought you were going to help for a few weeks?'

I took a deep breath and replied, 'So did I, but to be totally honest what I've just witnessed here today makes me feel very uncomfortable.'

49

Jo frowned. 'What do you mean?'

'The way you're carrying on.'

'What I do with my time is nothing to do with you.'

'That's correct, and I'm very pleased about that,' I said. 'How can you carry on with Ken, knowing your husband is very unwell and in hospital?'

'Me and Ken go back a long way.'

'Wonderful,' I said sarcastically. 'Let me tell you something, Jo. You don't mean anything to Ken. He was laughing at you walking down the stairs. You were just another notch in his belt. I came here today out of the goodness of my heart with the intention of helping you over Christmas. But I'm not helping you so that you have more time to jump in the sack with someone else while your husband's back is turned. I wouldn't be able to look him in the eye when he returned home.'

'Please yourself,' Jo sighed. Clearly she'd had this talk before – probably from Judith – and had ignored it.

On my way out, Judith said, 'I don't blame you. She's my sister, and I feel embarrassed by her. Mike could do much better than her, but the truth is he is besotted with her. He sees her through rose-tinted glasses. She can do no wrong in his eyes.'

'Do they have any children?' I asked.

'No,' said Judith.

'That's one good thing. It would be unfair to bring children up in that toxic environment.'

Judith went silent for a moment and then replied, 'I know what you have just said is probably right, but you see, the thing is, Jo can't have any children, and sometimes I think what she does is a way of punishing herself. I'm not making excuses – I still feel embarrassed – but she wasn't like that when she was younger. It's only in later life that she started sleeping around.'

I had that guilty feeling again.

Judith went on. 'I don't tell everyone what I've just told you, and the only reason I've told you is that I can see you are a really decent fella, probably from a very good family. You have been very kind, and I don't want you to leave with a really bad feeling towards my sister, just a bad feeling that I can live with, but not really bad. She was a good person once, but life has taken its toll.'

I thought for a moment. Perhaps I should go back. But the truth was I felt like this woman could have been my natural mum in another life. I knew she wasn't, but it felt too close to home, and I could not work with a woman who matches her standards. This wasn't my problem, and there wasn't any need for me to get any further involved. I could stand here and tell Judith my story, but what good would that do? It wouldn't help the situation. So I thanked Judith for her explanation and asked her to pass on my apologies for leaving. I wasn't sorry for what I said to Jo because it was the truth – I could see Ken laughing to himself at getting just another notch in his belt. And it wasn't the right thing to do when your husband was in hospital.

Judith shook my hand and said, 'Thanks for today. You've been so helpful.'

I needed to get home so I could clear my head.

*

My journey home didn't seem to take very long because I had so much to think about. I was relieved that I had left the pub; I know I couldn't stay there. I also realised that once I left the army I would need to be self-employed, as today's drama had really got the better of me.

Once I walked into my own home again I felt safe, and a great sense of relief came over me. I sat down, put the TV on and fell fast asleep until after midnight, when I woke up and took myself up to bed. The next morning I awoke feeling much better, with the hangover now fully behind me. I realised that it was Thursday, so only one more day until we would be meeting at Alex's place. Just then, there was a knock on the door – it was the delivery van with my rotary washing line, which was my job for the day – and to make sure the washing line stays up for more than one day.

I phoned Jon to ask if I could get a lift to Alex's place with him and Fay. I told him that he could pick me up from town, which was on his way, but he insisted he would pick me up from my place. May was also coming with us. I started to look forward to meeting Alex and his family, although I had already met Maria and she had left a lasting impression on me. I was looking forward to seeing her again, and I felt like I had a kind of VIP invitation, knowing that I had already met a family member. Best of all, I wondered to myself if I would have that butterfly feeling – or was that just a fleeting childish feeling? I didn't know, but I wouldn't have long to wait before I found out. I phoned Aunt Josephine later that day to make sure everything was still on for tomorrow, just in case. I also asked if there was anything she needed doing today as I was at a loose end.

'Yes, everything is set for tomorrow, and thank you for asking, but I have everything under control on my end today,' she said.

I enjoy having my own place, although it's not easy trying to get used to living on your own. My first week home had flown by, and after Christmas I would be back on duty for six to eight months. When I was home I did miss the daily routine of being on duty. I decided that when

I came home next time, I would start looking for a vehicle – and plumbing courses. In my mind, I had everything organised, and I just needed to put my plan into action once the time was right.

Chapter Four

⌒

The next day I was up bright and early. I went for a 10K run – I wanted to look my best for that evening. I couldn't help but think about Maria again. I hoped she would be the first person I saw. I imagined walking into the grand old house, and Maria and I would both be at the door, waiting to be welcomed in, and then we would walk towards the grand dining room, where the toastmaster would announce our names, and we would walk through the grand doors, and everybody would stand and clap and cheer us into the room, and this moment was filled with love and happiness. And both Maria and I would turn to look at each other with such admiration and devotion for each other, and a bond so strong that no one could break – it's eternal.

And then I woke up. I'm such a romantic sometimes. Wherever did I get this stuff from? I decided to live in hope for now.

After my 10k run, my next destination was a trip to the barber. I wasn't going to let Aunt Josephine down – I had to look my very best.

Right on cue Jon and Fay arrived at my place at 7 pm, then on to May's. Once we were all in the car nobody mentioned what we were doing, only what we'd been doing throughout the week. It didn't seem to concern anyone that we were going to be visiting Alex and his family – but then why would we worry when Aunt Josephine had made him sound like a perfectly down-to-earth person and a very hard-working man?

'Jesus, there's a gatehouse,' Jon exclaimed as we turned off the road. The gates were closed, so Jon drove up to them and pressed the intercom button and went to say something, but nothing came out. 'What should I say?' he whispered to Fay, panic setting in. 'How should I introduce us?'

Fay quickly said in an irritated tone of voice, 'Just tell them it's Jon!'

May laughed and said, 'Yes, just say your name. They know we're coming.'

'Hello, Jon here,' he said.

A reply came through: 'Yes, Jon.'

The gates buzzed and swung open, and we were in.

As we started up the driveway I felt like a VIP – it was all very grand. As we got nearer to the house we could see Aunt Josephine's car, so Jon parked alongside it, and we all got out. Just as we did that, a fellow came walking towards us. He had a nice smile, was tall and casually dressed.

'I'm Tom, Alex's son. Glad you could all make it. This is my wife Tiegan.' He gestured at the woman walking up behind him, who had two boys in tow.

'Hello, Tiegan,' we all said at exactly the same time.

The moment was so funny, and even Tiegan was laughing. It was like we were back in an assembly at school ('Good morning Mrs Tiegan, good morning everyone.')

Tiegan replied very casually, 'Just call me T.'

Tiegan was an instant hit, and I knew straight away I was going to get on with her. She had a kind smile and a beautiful tone of voice.

'And these are our sons,' Tom said, gesturing to the two boys who were, by now, standing up straight like little soldiers by his side. 'Alexander – he's nine – and Marcus, seven.'

They both held out their hands and we all shook hands. Marcus asked me if I was a real soldier. I knew then that Marcus was going to be my friend. Both boys were very well-mannered.

Jon held out his hand, and Tom shook both mine and Jon's hands and hugged May.

I had a quick look around to take in my surroundings. The house was very grand and looked very well kept.

Without thinking, I asked Tom, 'Is Maria here?'

Tom looked back at me and said, 'Have you met Maria?'

I thought to myself, *Why do I open my mouth?* 'Yes,' I replied. 'We met briefly in town.'

'Ah. No, Maria is running late. Being a journalist, something always comes up at the wrong time.'

I felt slightly disappointed for a moment.

Alex was waiting for us inside the house, but there was no sign of Aunt Josephine. I felt lost. Where was she? I had a thousand thoughts going through my mind like lightning. She'd told us that she and Alex were spending the day together; I hoped she was feeling okay.

Alex introduced himself and then showed us into the lounge. We were all taking in our surroundings, and then Khan, Linda, Indiana and Nevada arrived, along with Vy, who they'd picked up on the way. The girls were so excited – the house must have felt like a palace to them. Linda had dressed them so nicely, and I felt very proud of them both. But there was still no Josephine. Did I dare ask where she was? I decided I did.

'Where's Aunt Josephine?' I said.

Alex looked at me red-faced, which made me feel very uncomfortable.

No one else was part of the conversation, as Jon and Khan were chatting to Tom and T while they were busy organising drinks. Was I the only one who had noticed that Josephine wasn't with us?

Alex replied, 'Well, we had a bit of a disaster.'

My shirt started to feel very tight, and I felt rather hot under the collar.

The word 'disaster' finally made Khan and Jon turn around, so Alex now had our fullest attention. I thought to myself, You'd best get this right, Alex.

Alex explained. 'On the way back today, I ran over something in the road and punctured one of the tyres, and Josephine said, "We don't have time to wait for recovery. Let's change it ourselves," and I agreed. I got the spare tyre out from under the car – that's where it is, because it's a fairly old car. I passed it to Josephine, but it started to roll away. Josephine ran after the wheel and fell down into the ditch.'

We all looked shocked.

'Oh, she's okay,' Alex added quickly. 'Josephine didn't hurt herself, but she needed to shower and re-do her hair.'

I felt a sense of relief inside. So that's why she was running late.

Just a few minutes later, Aunt Josephine walked into the room looking very smart as always. She gave us all a kiss and thanked us for coming. Seeing Aunt Josephine in the grand surroundings made us all feel more comfortable.

The night went well. Alex cooked a lovely vegetable risotto, and the vegetables were all homegrown. Dessert was a pleasant surprise: no-frills jelly and ice cream. It went down a storm, especially with the kids.

After dinner, Alex FaceTimed Shannon in Los Angeles – it was around 12 noon there. Shannon looked delightful – she had an amazing smile with glowing white teeth and a mass of beautiful thick hair; the LA lifestyle definitely suited her. I felt like we were talking to a film star or an A-list celebrity because Shannon looked like a million dollars. I could see Alex was very proud of Shannon, as well as Maria and Tom.

After dinner, Tiegan showed May, Vy, Linda and the girls around the house, and Indiana and Nevada were still very excited. I could see Aunt Josephine was very happy with Alex. She had that youthful look about her, and it was lovely to see them together. Alex seemed a genuinely nice guy, despite my reservations in the beginning.

With still no sign of Maria – much to my dismay – we all moved into what looked like a very large lounge, which they called Monmouth suite. This room had four large settees, two armchairs, a large TV, a sound system and a very large open fireplace. We all made ourselves comfortable and Alex insisted we all have a drink, while the children settled down with a few board games.

After about an hour Khan decided it was time to go home as the girls were getting tired. Just as they were about to leave, Maria arrived. As she walked into the room, I felt the atmosphere lift. She looked straight at me, and for some silly reason I felt embarrassed, and I was unsure where to put myself for a brief moment. Then I told myself to grow up. It's hard to explain, and I think the answer is, now that I can look back, you know in your heart when you have found someone that you are really attracted to; it feels deeper than excitement. As I looked, everybody was standing still, waiting for Maria to say something. She looked around and said, 'I'm really sorry I didn't get here on time. Please forgive me.'

Maria looked at Khan and Linda and said, 'Please don't tell me you're leaving?'

Linda replied, 'The girls are getting really tired now, and we don't want to keep them up any longer.'

Maria looked at the girls. 'I'm so sorry for being so late, girls. What are your names?'

The girls told her, and Maria introduced herself in return.

Maria looked at Linda and said, 'You can stay the night if you want to.'

'That's very kind, Khan said, but tomorrow we're visiting Linda's parents, and we do have a fair way to travel, but thanks for asking – maybe next time.'

After Khan's family had said their farewells, Maria looked at the rest of us and said, 'I hope you're all staying?'

'We hadn't planned to,' May said.

'I spent all day yesterday getting the rooms ready,' Maria replied, and I could see that Maria was genuinely disappointed.

Vy said, 'I haven't got anything on tomorrow.'

Jon followed with the same response, and Fay and I looked at each other, shrugged our shoulders and both said, 'We don't mind,' followed by May. Maria looked relieved.

The rest of the night went well. We all had a few more drinks, and the atmosphere seemed to get very cosy. Maria put on some music, and we all had a dance. Soon Aunt Josephine, Alex, Tom, Tiegan and the boys had all gone to bed, and it was just me, Vy, May, Jon, Fay and Maria.

'When we were all younger,' Maria said, 'Granddad would get all the grandchildren together and in this very room we would all be singing and dancing. It was so much fun. My granddad was a lovely fellow. Not a week goes by when I don't think about him.'

Maria was really opening up. She told us that Josephine had made her dad a very happy man. 'It's lovely to watch them together. They're so compatible,' she remarked.

Jon told Maria, 'Josephine is a very hard-working, straightforward woman. Life hasn't been easy for her, and we all feared that she would get lonely once we all left home, so we as a family' – Jon looked around at us all – 'we as a family are very happy that they've found each other. And coming here tonight and seeing them together and meeting you, Tom, Tiegan and the boys, and seeing all the children together has all been so reassuring.'

I chimed in, 'We couldn't help but worry about Aunt Josephine, what with her being a woman on her own, after having had five children so being here, I feel, has been a relief.'

Maria told us that she and Tom felt exactly the same. Both Vy and May agreed. Maria told us that her dad was very happy with her mum, but her mum wasn't happy with being unable to fulfil her career. 'My mum always felt like this estate was holding her back, and Dad will never move on from this estate. My mum always tried to get him to sell up and move.'

Maria must have sensed that we were all trying to imagine why anyone would want to move away from such a beautiful place, so she continued, 'You see, Mum is a very wealthy woman in her own right.'

Maria's mum sounded very interesting, if I'm being honest, but I felt like Josephine should be the one and only. If I were to say that out loud, it would sound very childish, so I kept that to myself.

We all sat talking until the early hours of the next morning. It was very nice. Maria seemed a very nice person, just as I had imagined her. The butterflies had passed and I now felt very relaxed around Maria, which made her more attractive.

'So, what was going on at that pub?' she asked.

'Ever the journalist,' I replied, which made her laugh. 'I just helped out that morning.' I didn't feel like going into details. That morning was so full of drama from the very beginning, and my brain was in no mood to go over that again. So I changed the subject to something more interesting. 'Have you got a boyfriend?'

Vy said, 'Steady on, Sean. That's a bit personal, isn't it?'

'Or at least be politically correct,' Jon reminded me. 'You should have asked Maria if she has a partner.'

I hadn't considered Maria being gay, if I'm honest, and now that thought had entered my head I really hoped that Maria was straight.

I quickly replied, 'Okay, Jon. Sorry, Maria – have you got a partner?'

Maria smiled and replied, 'No, I'm not with anyone at this minute.'

This wasn't exactly the answer I wanted; I was hoping she would say no boyfriend. This was something of a dilemma. What should I ask next? I decided to be direct. 'Are you gay or straight?'

Maria was finding this all very funny. Maria replied, 'I haven't quite decided yet.'

'Wow, come on, give me a break,' I chuckled.

'You're going to have to work it out for yourself,' Maria replied sweetly.

Jon quickly changed the subject. 'Well, we've had a wonderful time here tonight in this grand old house. It's the perfect place for entertaining.'

Fay added, 'It's been lovely to see Alex And Josephine together. They look so happy.'

May said, 'Alex has made a new woman of our mother.'

Vy said, 'Your dad seems a genuinely nice fellow, and so long as our mother is happy, so are we.'

I finished the conversation by saying, 'Let's hope we have many more gatherings.' I looked straight at Maria as I spoke.

'I'll drink to that,' Maria said, clinking glasses with all of us.

At a little past 3 am we all said our goodnights, and Maria showed us all to the bedrooms.

'Is one of these bedrooms yours?' I asked Maria.

'I have a flat in one of the cottages near the greenhouse. It's only small but very comfortable. But I'm actually staying over here tonight so I can help Dad in the morning with breakfast.'

I replied, 'So, if I get scared, can I sleep in your room?'

'No,' she smiled. You stay in your own room.'

'Which one's your room?' I asked.

'That's for me to know and you to find out,' she quipped.

Jon said, 'Behave now, Sean.'

'Yes,' said May sternly.

'I'm only joking,' I replied.

'Well, it doesn't sound like that,' May said.

'Yep. Sounds like flirting,' Vy added. 'Please excuse our baby brother.'

Maria smiled and replied, 'It's okay. He's not my type.'

I felt like I was really out in the cold now, so even

though everyone was turning to head off to bed I replied, 'That remains to be seen.'

Everybody stopped and looked at me, including Maria, who had gone bright red.

'Sean, will you give up your flirting tonight please? Because you're not getting anywhere.'

'Your sister's right, Sean,' Maria said.

My name coming from her mouth felt like a small victory to me, and I laughed. 'Okay, let's call it a night.'

We all said our goodnights again, and that was the end of a wonderful evening. Gay or straight, I liked Maria very much and I felt a strong connection to her.

The room was very comfortable and well kept – not a speck of paint missing from the wall. All the rooms were ensuite and well-equipped. I got to bed, and my last thought was that I was looking forward to breakfast and chatting to Maria again.

*

The next morning was Saturday, and I remember thinking to myself how I hoped Aunt Josephine was still there, and hadn't gone off to the shop. Knowing her, she had probably got up before everybody else and gone to the shop and got back before we even knew she was gone.

When we got downstairs everything was laid out like we were in a hotel. The atmosphere had changed slightly – not in a bad way, just as if things had gone back to business, and that warm, homely, cosy feeling had turned more formal. I could see that this property was a mammoth task. Breakfast was served in the dining room, where we had eaten dinner the night before. I was the first downstairs, so I went into the kitchen, hoping to see Maria, but she wasn't there. The kitchen was very large and it was in two parts: one part had a feel of commercial catering about it, with large ovens and sinks and industrial-size hobs, large pots and pans; it reminded me of a military-style set-up. The other half was about half the size of the first, and it was a fitted kitchen in a very nice Victorian style; it looked pretty old but very well kept. Three women were in there, preparing breakfast. They looked about the same age as me, with very smart uniforms. As I walked in, they all turned and looked at me, and one of them asked if I was a member of Josephine's family.

I quickly replied, 'Yes, I'm Sean.'

'Pleased to meet you. We're the morning crew. I'm Willow, the head cleaner, and this is Martha – we call her the toilet inspector because cleaning the bathrooms is her speciality.'

Martha smiled and added, 'I cannot stand dirty toilets – or dirty anything, for that matter.'

And lastly, this is Tam. We call her Yum Yum, because she is the best chef around here.'

We chatted a while longer. All three women came across as being hard-working and very pleasant.

Tam asked if I would like a tea or coffee.

'Coffee please, Tam.'

She told me to go and make myself comfortable in the dining room and that she would bring it out to me.'

'No, it's okay – I'll take it with me. I'm not used to being waited on.'

Martha replied, 'Well, I'd make the most of it. This household doesn't carry any passengers. They'll soon have you working here.'

I laughed and replied, 'In that case, I'd better have double eggs with my breakfast.'

I went and sat down in the dining room, still on my own.

I thought to myself what a nice chat I'd had with the women. Willow, Martha and Tam all seemed very nice.

Settling into my chair, I looked around and the word 'splendid' entered my head – a word that I wouldn't normally use but that felt perfect for the setting.

Just then, Alex walked in, dressed very smartly. He had the air of a sergeant major about him, just that look of authority.

'Morning, Sean. Did you sleep well?'

Without thinking, I replied, 'Yes, sir— I mean Alex.'

Alex asked me, 'Have you got much on today?'

I replied, 'Yes. I'm heading over to Khan's house, and I'm supposed to be building a den for the girls for Christmas.'

'That's a splendid idea.'

I thought to myself how 'splendid' was my word, and I smiled.

'Yes, I think so. How about you, Alex? Have you got much on today?'

Alex replied, 'Yes. We have a meeting booked at noon, with a light lunch – sandwiches, finger buffet, you know, that sort of thing – and then the Monmouth suite, the room we were all in after dinner last night, that's booked for an anniversary party. And that's without the visitors to the grounds today. This place is like a treadmill that never stops.'

I asked Alex, 'Do you have any time when the house is not being used?'

Alex nodded his head and replied, 'Yes, after New Year's Day we officially close the house for around six weeks, but that's when we get all the maintenance done, so nearly every day there will be a tradesman working in the house. We never really get to have the house to ourselves very much. Last night was the first time in a long time – that's why Maria was happy that you all stayed over. It takes all of us to run this place. Tom, Tiegan and Maria all have to help out. My oldest daughter, like my wife, couldn't wait to get away from this place.'

I must have had a look of disbelief on my face because Alex added, 'Having a place like this, on this scale, is a prison sentence, believe me. It's nice to say this is where I live, but the actual reality of living in a place like this is exhausting. I inherited the estate from my family. I'm the sixth generation to live here, and I don't want to be the one to lose it. I hardly stop working, and when I'm not working I'm trying to come up with new ideas to earn money and keep up with the modern world.

'Sounds tough. I don't suppose you get much time for holidays?' I ventured.

'It's possible, but when you're living in a venue environment as splendid as this one, what can compare to this? So again the chains of this estate fit tight around my neck. I myself have to play a part and even dress for the role, just like an actor. People who visit here and rent the rooms all have their own ideas and expectations of what they want this place to be and feel like, and we can't afford to let them down, not least because we now have best friends called Facebook, Tripadvisor etc, so it can feel like you're walking a tightrope at times. The best thing is renting out like the farms we have, however the house and the grounds are different because I know if I rent those out, the tenants would just bleed the property dry. They wouldn't want to put any money back in like I do.'

I was shocked, and Alex could see that. He went on.

'Sixty-eight per cent of the money generated by this estate goes back into the property, and that's why we have to keep finding new ways to make money, so we ourselves can have a decent standard of living. I also try myself – along with Tom, T and Maria – to do as much maintenance and groundwork as physically possible, to save money. People have said to me in the past, "You were born with a silver spoon in your mouth," and from the outside I suppose that's just what it looks like, but for me and my family, it feels more like a tool kit.'

Alex was very interesting to listen to and very straightforward in what he was saying. He was no bullshit lord of the Manor, and if I'm honest that's just what I was expecting. Alex fulfilled all

my expectations – that was for sure. Aunt Josephine had painted a clear picture of him.

Just then, Josephine, Vy and May walked in, and Tam brought in more tea and coffee while Willow brought in breakfast for everyone. Minutes later, Jon and Fay walked in, followed by Tom, Tiegan and the boys – but no Maria.

I asked Alex if Maria had been called out.

'No. She'll be here in a moment. She's gone to check today's agenda for me, so that I don't miss anything.'

Josephine walked in, and as usual, she had no time to chat – it was Saturday morning, and she needed to get to the shop. For a brief moment, it felt like we were back together in our old family home. We all finished breakfast and started to think about what was next for the day ahead. I had a den to make, but I wanted to see Maria before I left, because I enjoyed flirting with her.

Eventually Jon stood up and said, 'Well, Alex, Tom, Tiegan, it's been a great privilege to have met you all, and thank you for your hospitality, and we hope that we all get many more opportunities like this.'

Alex and Tom thanked Jon and agreed.

I felt like I still needed to see Maria, and I wondered to myself if she felt the same. Maybe I wasn't right for her and that was why she hadn't bothered to come and see us before we left. I felt disappointed, in all honesty. Maybe she was gay and didn't want to lead me up the garden path. In all fairness, that was the right approach, so I can't be disappointed, and I should be grateful. So, I didn't say anything, I just picked up my disappointment, got back in the car and we all left.

*

Later that day, I made my way to Khan's place. They have a lovely home – Linda has beautiful taste, and everything is so clean, although it still manages to be really homely, and you're at home as soon as you put your foot through the door. I could have snuggled up on their settee and watched TV all day, to be honest, because I was still tired from the night before, and even a cold shower hadn't livened me up, but I needed to build the den while the girls were visiting their grandparents. I opened the door and a beautiful fresh clean smell hit me straight in the face, and it seemed to beg me to come straight in and sit down. I don't know how Linda does it but she has to be one of the best housekeepers ever. I got stuck straight in to making the den because I knew that if I sat down even for one minute in this beautiful, comfortable, well-kept house I would go straight to sleep.

I unlocked Khan's shed, which – thanks to Khan being a self-employed electrician – was full of everything I'd need to make the den. As promised, Khan had partitioned off part of the garden creating a hidden part of the garden next to the wall – a great idea, because it only needed two sides. The wood had been delivered, and Khan had also ordered some large wooden fence posts, which he told me to put in the ground first; I would need to dig down by about a metre in order for this idea to work. I had imagined it would be easier than that. I stood staring at the materials for some time.

Then it came to me. I remembered how, when I was about fourteen, I got a job at the fair, helping out with the stalls. The guy I'd worked for called the round stall the hoopla, and he had three of them to pack away. I hadn't helped set up, but I did help to take them down. When we took them down I remembered thinking how clever it was how they fixed together. And that was just how I was going to put the den together. This idea was perfect.

I marked out where to put the fence posts. I then went into the shed and found some L-shaped brackets and drilled holes in them so that I could put a hook through. After this, I fixed hooks on what was going to be the roof beams, just the same as the hoopla idea, so you put the hook into an eyelet, and as I lifted the roof beam up straight the hook would curl round the eyelet and hold it in place; then the other end of the roof bream would need another eyelet and hook. This way, as I lifted the wooden fence post up straight to place in the ground, both hooks would be curled around the eyelets to hold it firmly in place. By using this idea I wouldn't need any help to put it up. I needed three roof beams, and once I got the frame up I need to cut the wood the make cross beams to hold the den firmly in place, and once again I made hooks and eyelets, which made the structure much stronger. My little job on the fair as a young lad had stood me in good stead. Khan would be very impressed, I'm sure.

I managed to finish the frame, but by then it was getting

dark so I couldn't finish the whole den. I left it partitioned off, so the girls wouldn't see it. Before I went back inside I noticed my boots had gotten a bit dirty, so to avoid upsetting Linda I cleaned the boots. Even though we take our shoes off indoors, I didn't even want to carry my dirty boots through Linda's immaculate home. Next, I made myself a cup of tea and put the telly on. I must have fallen fast asleep because the next thing I remember was the sound of the girls running up the stairs.

Khan and Linda walked into the lounge.

'How did you get on?' Khan asked.

'Pretty good, I reckon,' I said. 'Wait – what time is it?'

'Eight.'

'Oops. I've got to get going. I'll miss the last bus.'

Linda said, 'Why don't you stay? You can finish the den tomorrow, and you can stay for dinner.'

'Are you sure?'

Linda rolled her eyes and laughed. 'I wouldn't have said it if I wasn't sure.'

'I don't feel like moving anyway, to be honest,' I conceded. 'Thanks, Linda. You're a star.'

'Beer?' Khan said.

'No, not tonight, thank you. We had enough last night.'

'What time did you get to bed?' asked Khan.

'About 3 am.'

'No wonder you're tired!' Khan sat down beside me and went on. 'Maria seemed nice. We were sorry that we needed to leave. I would have liked to have stayed.'

'We had a good night, to be fair. Maria is very nice.'

Khan smiled. 'You took a shine to her?'

'Well, I bumped into her before last night, to be honest, and she kind of left an impression.'

Khan replied, 'I could see that when I mentioned her name.'

I smiled.

'You really like her. I can see it.'

'I'm very attracted to her, I have to admit that much. But I can see she doesn't feel the same.'

'And how do you know that?' asked Khan.

I took a deep breath. 'I'm not sure whether Maria is gay or straight.'

'Have you asked her?'

'Yes.'

'Really?' Khan replied, 'What did she say?'

'I didn't get a straightforward answer.'

'Well, the question is very personal,' Khan mused. 'I see what you mean though. That is a dilemma.'

Linda had overheard our conversation and said, 'If you like Maria, Sean, the only way around this is for you to get to know her.'

'I will try and get to know Maria better if I get the opportunity.'

'When did you first meet Maria?'

I decided that I wasn't going over that drama again, so I just explained I'd bumped into her in the Coach Inn.

Linda's eyes lit up. 'Oh, I know that pub – the landlord Mike is a lovely fellow – too nice, in fact.' I felt saddened, and Linda must have seen the look on my face. 'You okay, Sean?' she asked.

I quickly replied, 'I'm okay, but Mike has had a heart attack. I'm sorry to have to tell you.'

Linda went pale.

Khan asked, 'Is that the Mike you went to school with?'

'Yes,' Linda replied quietly. 'I'll phone his sister

tomorrow.' She looked at me again. 'How did you find out, Sean? That Mike had a heart attack?'

'I just happened to be in the pub the day before, and I left my shopping in there, and when I went back the next day his wife Jo told me. I'm sorry, Linda.'

Linda replied, 'I'm glad you told me, Sean.'

Khan turned the conversation back around to Maria. 'So, how can we arrange for you and Maria to meet up again?'

I shook my head and said, 'I have no idea.'

Khan looked at me sternly. 'What do you mean? Come on, Sean. You will have to do better than that if you think you might have feelings for Maria.'

I took in what Khan said and replied, 'Okay', but deep down I was concerned in case I wasn't her type. Rejection wasn't something that I could take lightly – but then again I suppose most people think like that; chances are put before us so that we can take them, and how we deal with that chance depends mostly on our attitudes. I knew that I liked Maria, and I knew that I was attracted to her, so the best thing I could do was follow my heart and keep a level head. I was going to ride this wave.

I answered Khan, 'I suppose you're right. It's not like I have anything to lose.'

Khan smiled and replied, 'That's right. You will never know if you don't try.'

With that thought locked in my head, I changed the subject. 'How has your day gone?'

'We have had a nice day. Linda's parents are well. We also called in and saw Father.'

My stomach flipped. 'How's he keeping?' I asked, reluctantly.

'He looked very well, until I told him about Alex. He didn't take that too well.'

'You told him?!'

'Yes, because I didn't want anybody else telling him. The last thing Mother needs right now is Father on a bad day.'

'How did he take it?'

'He didn't say a great deal at first, but once the idea sunk in, Father told me that he hoped that Mother was happy. He said, "Josephine has done everything right, and if anybody deserves to be happy it's her – unlike me. I messed everything up." Father told me that he was grateful that Mother had done such a good job of bringing us all up. It's only right that she finds happiness.'

Just to be polite, I asked, 'How's Father doing?'

'Not brilliant, but he looks okay. He's still working in the garage. They've moved him off the night shifts. Now he works from 1 pm to 9 pm six days a week, and that keeps him out of trouble, pays the bills and keeps the wolves at bay.'

I was glad when the conversation was over and we moved on. I wasn't that interested in talking about Father, if I'm totally honest. I just show interest for Khan's benefit because he shows interest and concern for all the family and has all of our best interests at heart. And him making sure Father knew about Alex benefits both him and Josephine.

Chapter Five

∞

The next morning I woke early. I stayed in the spare room, which is more comfortable than my bedroom at my place. I don't know how Linda keeps everything so perfect – I thought Josephine was the best, but Linda is way in front, and her attention to detail is second to none. Khan is a very good husband and loves all the attention to detail himself. Both Khan and Linda are experts at making the most of what they have. Linda doesn't go out to work – her job is a stay-at-home mum and housekeeper. If you asked me if Khan's a wealthy man, I would reply yes, very wealthy: wealth in health, wealth in love, wealth in loyalty, wealth in honesty, wealth in happiness, all of which makes for a good life, and a very wealthy man. Technically, Khan's life is very middle class, but the standard seems higher. Josephine made sure that we all understood the importance of good living, and it didn't mean having lots of money.

Thinking back, I remember when our sofa was completely worn out, and it was coming up to Christmas. Josephine always worked hard to make Christmas special in the 'togetherness' way. I remember her telling Khan that she needed to do something with that sofa ready for Christmas.

Khan replied, 'Can we buy a new sofa?'

'We don't need a new sofa.' Josephine said. 'The frame is still very strong. We just need it re-upholstered.'

At the time I didn't know what she meant. After that conversation, the sofa disappeared. I was too young and didn't take any notice. Then one day I got back from school and our sofa had returned. Josephine and Khan had taken their time and completely re-upholstered it, and now it was as good as new. It lasted right up until Josephine sold the house. That's how we were all brought up, but Khan is slightly better than the rest of us at upcycling. Khan can upcycle most things and leave no trace of their past.

That morning after breakfast I noticed Khan in the garden inspecting the den, so I walked over and joined him. He told me he was very impressed with how I had put it together. That morning I needed to fit the camouflage canvas cover, and I wanted it to be as watertight as possible. Khan suggested that we wrap the canvas cover around the wooden beams and screw the canvas underneath, because that way the water should fall away before it reaches the screw head. Knowing how screwheads can hold water, I thought this to be the most suitable way to fit the canvas cover to the frame, so I agreed.

After breakfast, we set about fitting the canvas cover. There was enough cover to go right over the top and down the sides; Khan didn't want it to be completely covered around the bottom because he still want to be able to get the lawn mower in and around the den to keep it tidy. There wasn't any need to cut the cover as it fitted very well. However – typical for him – Khan wanted to make the best ever den known to man. He wanted the top fitted separately to the sides because if there were strong winds they would only affect either the top or the sides. I suppose he was right, but this made it a much bigger job.

We started with the top. We marked out every millimetre to prevent any wastage, making sure we had allowed enough fabric to wrap around the beams. Then I spotted a problem. 'Wait a minute – how will we fit the cover to the centre beam?'

Khan thought for a moment before saying, 'If we wrap it tight enough around the end beams, that should hold it firmly in place.'

We managed to fit the camouflage canvas almost perfectly. This den would be fit for our little princesses, that was a sure thing. By dinner time, the canvas roof was fitted and it looked amazing.

Dinner at Khan and Linda's was as always delicious, but this time not only was the dinner delicious but the table was laid out fit for the Queen, and that's how you make the best of what you have. We could have been having dinner in a six-star hotel and it wouldn't have looked any better. I felt like I needed to put on my suit – not in a stiff, uncomfortable way but in a polite way, as a nod to the effort Linda had made.

I couldn't wait to get started back on the den. The sides were going to be easier because the roof hung over both sides by about twelve inches. We carried on, and like we did with the roof we wrapped the cover around the wooden fence posts and screwed the canvas cover on the inside so that when the rain fell there wasn't anything to stop the flow of water. Then to make sure the den was secured to the brick wall we wrapped the canvas around two pieces of timber the same length as the den and screwed them to the wall – perfect.

Next, the front. We thought it would be a brilliant idea if we did the front like curtains so that in the summer it could be more like a shelter, and if it rained or it was colder you could drop the curtains down.

By the end of the day, the den was fully built. All that was left was adding the bits of furniture that I'd bought – the little table and chairs, the battery lights and solar panels. Once the decorations were all in place, I stuck the old records and CDs to the walls and they looked really effective.

We had enough wood left over to make a bookshelf for the den. Khan took over this job because he wanted to sand down the shelves and varnish them so they would be more weather-resistant. I had one last look at our work before I made my way home – by then it was just starting to get dark so I tried the battery lights, and I have to say the den looked a real treat – I was chuffed. I left Khan's place knowing that the girls would be very pleased with the den.

*

Christmas came around pretty quickly. Christmas Day was organised by Khan and Linda, and it was nothing less than perfect. The best part for me came after dinner, when we all gathered in the garden and Khan took down the partition for the grand reveal of the den. The girls' faces lit up. They were amazed and so excited. In fact, they were so excited that they found it hard to focus on what they actually had, and their emotions were running high. Josephine, Vy, May and Jon were also very impressed, and in fact at one point we were all inside the cosy den.

We decided to go back indoors and let the girls settle down. Once they were calmer, they asked me if I had really made the den.

'Yes – with help from your dad.'

'It's the best present I've ever had,' Nevada told me.

'Can we take another look?' Indiana asked.

The three of us went back into the garden, and this time the girls were more focused. They asked how I made the den and where I bought all the decorations from. I went over everything and made sure they understood that most of the articles were reclaimed rather than new. The girls were truly delighted with the den and couldn't thank me enough for coming up with such a good idea.

The evening passed quickly and before long we all went our separate ways. I had arranged to meet up with Sophie and Paul, and Vy and May were going off with their friends. Linda's parents were making their way over to Khan and Linda's place for Christmas tea. Jon and Fay were entertaining at their place – which I was invited to but I had made my own my plans. Alex was due to pick up Josephine, then they would also head over to Jon's place.

Christmas had come around quickly and it had gone just as quickly, and in fact, New Year's Eve did the same. I didn't go out to celebrate it because everyone was coming to my place on New Year's Day and I wanted it to be special, so I spent all of New Year's Eve preparing my place. There were going to be at least eleven of us, plus I had also invited Tom, Tiegan, their boys, and Maria. Tom and Tiegan had declined became they were entertaining, but Maria had said she would do her best to get there but not to make any preparation for her – in other words, not to worry about getting food in for her. I really hoped she would make it; it would be another opportunity to get to know her.

The forecast was dry, so I came up with the idea of having a barbecue. A first I thought my idea was a bit wild, but as I put more thought into it I decided it was a really good plan. All the food would be cooked outside and I could lay out a buffet in the kitchen so that everyone could help themselves. The more I thought about my idea, the more I liked it.

I went to the garden centre and asked if they had any barbecues left. The woman was very helpful: not only did they have barbecues but they were reduced. She took me round to the back room and there was everything I needed. I chose a barbecue, and then a patio set caught my eye. It was an L-shaped sofa and a large table with some chairs – ideal for me. I also noticed an outdoor heater and decided I had to have it, especially at 50% off. I spent £750.00, which was a lot more than I expected to spend, but I had actually got about £1,500 worth of equipment so I thought this to be a very good deal.

The garden centre delivered everything the next day. When it arrived it looked very nice and much to my delight everything I bought came with winter covers, which is just as well as I'd never even given that a thought. The day before New Year's Eve I'd gone to the butcher and told him my plan.

'Good idea!' he said. 'Leave it with me. Can you come back tomorrow at about 2 pm and I will have everything you need for eleven people at a barbecue.'

I left him to it – what a weight off my shoulders. Then I called in at our local shop and picked up everything I needed to make a salad, plus Greek salad for a change. And with that, I was organised.

May and Vy were coming over early to give me a hand. May was also bringing her boyfriend, Jeff. I think this is his first mention because it's been an on–off relationship for the past six years and to tell the truth it's a bit difficult to get interested, and the family just doesn't bother to ask any more. If I'm totally honest, I think Jeff is gay, and going out with May is his way of trying to please his mum and dad. I believe May knows this and is being too nice. I've never mentioned this to anyone; it's just my thoughts. I do get on okay with Jeff and so does Jon, but Khan doesn't – he's never mentioned it to me, but his body language says it all.

*

The big day arrived, and I was more than ready. My sisters arrived early as promised, and we did the preparations, and then it was time to party. The barbecue idea went down a storm – everybody kept telling me what a good idea it was. Everything got eaten, plus the indoors/outdoors idea was great because we weren't all sitting on top of each other. Aunt Josephine told me she was very impressed with everything I had done, which pleased me a great deal. The only dampener, I thought as I nursed my drink, was that Maria hadn't turned up. I knew she wasn't a definite yes, but as I sat there in conversation with Fay, my mind drifted to the possibility that Maria wasn't interested in me. Perhaps I should put my attention elsewhere.

And, of course, just as this was going through my mind, Maria walks in.

That time, I didn't make any fuss, just sat there as cool as cucumber, continuing my conversation with Fay. Maria looked straight at me, and I just raised my hand and nodded my head. By the look on her face, this wasn't the reaction she wanted, but I decided that if I made a fuss it wouldn't get me anywhere.

I shouldn't have doubted myself as it was clear from the moment she walked in that we were attracted to each other – that I know for sure. I hoped we could build on that.

After a few minutes, we gravitated towards each other and started to talk, which was great. However, my mood changed slightly, if I'm honest, once the conversation moved on to her sexuality; it made me think that maybe she wasn't attracted to me and that this was her way of letting me down softly. Some women just truly enjoy flirting, I know, but I was still attracted to Maria and I sincerely hoped she was looking for a boyfriend. I supposed boyfriend sounded a bit childish, so maybe man-friend might be the answer. After taking in the look on Maria's face I wasn't going to move.

A few minutes later, May steered Maria into the kitchen to get something to eat and drink. I sat down next to Linda for a chat – nothing of great interest but we were both comfortable and the atmosphere was relaxed, so her company was enjoyable. After some time Maria and May reappeared from the kitchen. Maria had a drink and a plate, and I felt pleased because I could see she was comfortable. Both women sat down, carrying on their conversation, and I sensed Maria casually glancing my way, which made me feel warm inside – a real sense of contentment. I hardly knew Maria, but she had some kind of magic over me, that I felt for sure.

The day had gone well and everybody had enjoyed themselves. Khan and Linda left early, but Jon, Fay, May, Vy, Alex and Josephine were all staying over, while Jeff made his excuses and left. Jon turned his hand to making cocktails for everyone, and he'd brought in some ingredients and a recipe book for the cocktails. We had the best time. I felt on top of the world; I was so pleased with myself for having my own place. Looking around the room and watching everybody enjoying themselves gave me a sense of achievement. All my years of service – all the sweat and hard work – were worth it.

It wasn't long before Maria and I were sitting very

comfortably on the sofa. Maria was telling me all about her work and what was going on in town. Maria was very interesting: she was a wealth of information, and there wasn't much that Maria didn't know. I was very impressed, to be honest, as she knew about new developments, council news, even some criminal news, and road traffic accidents. Not much got past Maria, that was for sure.

Into the small hours, everyone started to go off to sleep wherever they were comfortable, so we decided it was bedtime. Maria went upstairs to crash with May and Vy in my room, and Josephine and Alex were given the spare room. Jon, Fay and I made good use of the sofa and chairs.

The next morning I woke up early and got everything tidy before anybody else woke up; I wanted to make sure everyone was as comfortable as possible. Before long the barbecue was going again – this time for bacon and mushroom sandwiches, and plenty of coffee all round.

When everyone was getting ready to leave, Maria came up to me. 'What are you doing today?' she asked casually.

'Are you asking me out?' I quipped.

She smirked. 'Yes. Of course I am.'

I tried to stay cool. 'It's New Year's Day – where can we go?'

Maria thought for a moment and said, 'Do you fancy ice skating?'

'Yes – are you thinking Cardiff winter wonderland?'

She nodded.

'That sounds great, but how will we get there today?'

'I can drive,' she said.

'Ice skating?' Jon echoed, and he looked at Vy excitedly.

So, it ended up being a group of us, but we had a great afternoon. Cardiff winter wonderland is a great day out, even though none of us could skate, so all we did was laugh. It was so much fun, and I loved being in Maria's company. She was so pleasant, very well mannered and just great to be with. And that day was the day I finally established that she wasn't gay, so then I knew I was in with a chance, I was sure of it.

Towards the end of the day, when no one else was around, I asked Maria if I could take her out – maybe this time without any other family members.

A big smile appeared on her face, which felt amazing. I had that butterfly feeling again; the only way I can describe the feeling is magic.

We met a few times after that, and we just hit it off – the magic was there from the start and we both knew it.

*

The days flew by, and the time came for me to go back on duty – and this time I would be gone for eight months. We promised each other that we would keep in touch, and I felt sure that wouldn't be a problem. I had made arrangements for my place to be temporarily rented out through the local agency – a suggestion from a friend. I didn't love the idea, but I liked it more than the house sitting empty for so long.

The day arrived and it was time for me to leave. I dropped my keys at the estate agent, who'd assured me that they would take good care of my property. I let them know that my sisters would need to have access for the fitting of my curtains and blinds, and then I made my way back to the barracks.

For the first time ever, I felt reluctant to go back on duty. My life was starting to change in a positive way, and I was enjoying the change. Maria and I had managed to get together twice before I left. We were only talking, getting to know each other better, but that was good enough for me; I was very happy just in her company. She made me feel on top of the world. For some strange reason anything felt possible – that's how I felt when I was with Maria.

In the briefing I was informed I could be gone for eight to nine months. I hoped it would be eight. The time went quickly though – Maria and I kept in touch. For the first time I felt like I had two lives – a life on duty and a life at home – and I was starting to prefer my home life. This helped me make a firm decision that I was going to become a plumber, and when I got home I planned to start the course. Maria was keeping me up to speed with what was going on at home, which was a first for me. I'd spent all that time in the forces, but never before had I received a letter from a girlfriend. Maria is a very good writer – she knows just how to put words together to grab your attention. The word 'journalist' had never entered my thoughts before, but my god, Maria has a wealth of knowledge and information; in fact, I think everyone should know a journalist.

I focused on my job and it didn't seem too long before I was considering my return. The eight months did turn into nine in the end, but it wasn't a problem, and soon I was looking at just two weeks left before I was going home, and I started to make plans and look forward to it.

*

I landed back in my home life finally, and I was looking forward to a few days' stay at Josephine's, which she insisted upon so she could pamper me and allow me to catch up on rest. My first stop was Josephine's shop, where she was busy at work as always. I was so glad to see her.

She gave me a hug. 'I'm glad you're home.'
I hugged back. 'Me too.'

'How much longer will you be in the army?'

'One year, three months.' I knew the exact answer because I'd double-checked before I left. I wasn't going to be home for Christmas this year, and I broke this news to Josephine.

'Well, we all had a good time this year, so we'll have to be grateful,' she said kindly.

I was very excited about my leave time because I needed to organise my course. I'd asked for extra time off, so I had a full ten weeks' leave ahead of me, and I had lots of things to sort out.

Josephine's shop was next to our old family home, and I couldn't help stopping to have a look to see if the new owners had changed anything – which they had. All the front windows had been changed, which made the house look modern and up to date. As I stood there, my childhood memories came flooding back, and that made me feel very happy.

I hoped my place was all okay and that my cosy home had been put to good use while I was away. The estate agents had seemed pretty confident that they could find a few temporary lets. I considered the possibility of some damage, which I had been warned about and was always a risk with renting, but the estate agent guaranteed that they would collect a substantial deposit in case there was any problem with any tenant. Aunt Josephine didn't like the idea, but I thought it was great because it helped out with the mortgage, which meant I could save my money.

That day was really full-on, and Josephine and I went out for dinner that night, after which I collapsed into the indescribably cosy bed she'd made up for me.

The next day my attention turned to Maria – I wanted to see her, and I hoped we could pick up where we'd left off.

We'd stayed in touch throughout my absence, and she hadn't given me any indication that anything was going to change, but I still felt anxious and really wanted to see her. But first, I had a few things to sort out.

I was up early, and I went for a 10K run, and then I got myself cleaned up and went to the estate agents. The guy who had taken the keys from me and sorted out the contracts wasn't around, and his colleagues couldn't access his computer to get my file. They didn't say as much, but I think he had left.

One of the staff, Debbie, informed me that she hadn't been sure of my return date, and so my place was still occupied by the current tenants. I felt very disappointed by this information and Debbie noticed my reaction and assured me everything would be fine, but that I couldn't have the keys back until the end of the month – eight more days.

I wasn't pleased, but there was nothing I could do about the present situation. I decided then and there that I'd never rent out my place again. I didn't care how much money I stood to get; I wanted my place back. The guy I dealt with first promised £4,500, but that was of no interest to me when I had no home to move back into when I needed it.

I went back to Aunt Josephine's place. I really didn't want to tell her the news, but there wasn't any choice. I know she wouldn't mind me staying with her, but I knew she would be worried about my place in case anything had gone wrong, so I decided not to tell her too much, especially about the estate agent who had left.

Now for my next task, and the one I was most looking forward to: I made contact with Maria. She answered her phone before it had the chance to ring, which I thought was a very good sign. I could tell by the tone of her voice she was pleased that I was home. We made arrangements to meet up in two days – on Friday – and I booked the Italian restaurant for 8 pm. I felt very pleased that I would be meeting Maria again and I hoped that she felt the same. Once the plans were made, all I could think about was Friday. I thought of all the things to talk about, and I'd even practised my conversations in the mirror, because I just wanted everything to be perfect.

*

Friday came around and I got to the restaurant half an hour early because I felt so anxious. I decided to have a drink before Maria arrived, to calm myself down. Maria arrived she looked stunning I had never seen her dress in this style before, gone were her casual clothes, Maria was wearing a beautiful lemon-coloured dress, the only way I can describe this dress was brazier style double breasted with a white belt, bag and shoes, which contrasted with her dark skin – she looked perfect. Her hair was no longer tied up – she had let it down – and I had never seen her legs before. It was a good job I was sitting down and had managed to get a drink down, otherwise I think I would have fallen over. I felt like John Travolta in *Grease*, when he sees Olivia Newton-John in her new outfit – it was very clear to both of us that we were happy to see each other again.

'Wow ... Wow,' was all I could say, then blurted out, 'You look amazing.'

'You look pretty handsome yourself, Lance Corporal Arrowsmith.'

The sound of Maria's voice addressing me by my rank sent a tingle down my spine and made me feel very proud of myself. Just that one sentence made it worth all the work.

The conversation flowed throughout the evening, and the food went down a treat. We had a few drinks and we both felt relaxed, so much so that Maria suggested we walk round to the hotel for a drink before we called it a night. I didn't want this night to end I've never felt as comfortable as I feel with Maria, so I eagerly agreed. As we walked round to the Hotel Maria held out her hand so I took it. I really wanted to wrap my arms around her and tell her how beautiful she looked, but I held back. I didn't want to spoil the moment. I felt on top of the world.

We got to the hotel and sat down, and the bartender walked over to take our order. I had never been to this hotel before, it was all very nice, quite upmarket. We sat talking about our families and work, and we seemed to have a lot in common. I felt I could have sat chatting with Maria for the rest of my life. I loved how she could see the funny side of things, and she was very witty, so we weren't short on laughter.

Then after one too many drinks, I had this overwhelming feeling come over me. I needed to pull myself together before Maria noticed. I wasn't sure what it was – perhaps a sense of achievement about being with Maria? I couldn't put my finger on the exact reason, but I suppose it was a combination of everything.

It was getting late and time to start thinking about leaving, but neither I nor Maria wanted to leave. Still, I was shocked when Maria suggested we stay the night. I was very happy just being in her company, but it was very clear she was happy to move the relationship to the next stage – which was fine with me. I had never felt like this with any other woman, and it wasn't just about the sex, but rather not wanting to leave each other.

I walked to reception and asked if they had any rooms available, but I came to a stop before I reached the desk. I felt a bit seedy if I'm honest, as if this wasn't good enough for Maria, so I changed my mind.

'None available,' I told Maria as I returned to the bar. I felt awkward about the lie, but it felt right.

I did sense a look of slight relief on Maria's face at this news, so I was really glad I had changed my mind. We had something special, and I wasn't prepared to take any chances.

I suggested we go back to Aunt Josephine's and crash there. We could walk to Josephine's from the hotel, and that's just what we did. Once we got to Josephine's I made coffee and toast, and we sat chatting until the early hours. Maria had my room, and I slept on the sofa.

Once we said good night I got comfortable and I started to think about our night out. It was great – we had delicious food, good drinks and never-ending conversation. I thought about my decision at the hotel. Of course, I would have enjoyed spending the night with Maria – I'm a man, and I felt like I could have made love to her all night. After all, Maria was so beautiful. However, I felt a very deep connection with her and wasn't going to take any chances. I could see Maria was trying to please me, but in my opinion, a woman as nice as Maria doesn't have to please me. She is intelligent enough to just please herself, and only that can make me happy. We would both know when the time is right. And with that in mind, I fell fast asleep.

The next morning I awoke to the sound of Josephine making us a cup of tea. Maria got up and made herself comfortable next to me on the sofa. I felt such contentment that I didn't want the morning to end. Maria had the day off, so before Josephine left for the shop she sorted out some casual clothes for Maria to wear, and luckily enough they were the same shoe size.

We chilled out, just watching TV until lunchtime when we decided to go down to the deli for a sandwich and coffee. They know what they're doing at that deli: their coffee is the best, and the delicious smell hits you the moment you walk through the door, like the cold air on a frosty morning. There is no chance that you would ever leave the deli without a cup of coffee in your hand.

*

The next few weeks saw me and Maria spending most of our time together. My first job was to get my house back – but that didn't work out the way I had hoped. I picked up the keys with no problem, but when I walked in through my front door, the first thing I noticed was a terrible smell. Then I saw they had left lots of rubbish behind. I was extremely disappointed. The estate agent had promised the place would be left how it was found, and that clearly wasn't the case. I phoned the estate agent, but – rather conveniently for them – they weren't picking up. There was nothing else to do but get on the job myself.

I phoned the carpet cleaner and took down the curtains – it was the first time I'd seen them and they were already filthy – I took them to the dry cleaners. Within a few days, I got the place back up to scratch, and then my next job was to retrieve the money they'd promised.

I was expecting just under £5,000 as my reward for letting out my house. After I finished the cleaning I paid a visit to the estate agents. The guy I first dealt with still wasn't around, and Debbie still couldn't access his computer. Before I left I told them I wanted my money transferred as soon as possible. The guy had promised me when I dropped off the keys that my money would be paid into my account monthly, I didn't have time to chase it up while I was away. I left the estate agents with nothing more than a bunch of excuses and a few weak promises from Debbie. It was looking very suspicious, and I felt very concerned that I wasn't going to get my money.

I didn't tell anyone about the tenancy issue because I didn't want anyone to worry, especially Josephine. After a week or two and still no money, I decided to forget it. My many visits to Debbie had gotten me nowhere, and I had better things to spend my time on. Maria and I were spending more and more time together, and it was working out very nicely. I felt so good about us that I asked Maria if she wanted to visit the Lake District with me over the third weekend in October because I wasn't going to be around for Christmas. Maria agreed and we made the arrangements.

Chapter Six

❦

Three weeks after I gave up chasing Debbie, the money from the estate agents landed in my bank account. It was £500 short, but I didn't make any fuss because I considered myself lucky to have got that. The money came in very handy for my plumbing course, which I found pretty easy and sailed through. I put that down to the fact that I already had some experience in plumbing through the army. I still needed a van, but I wasn't going to purchase that until I returned the next time.

The third weekend in October came around very quickly, and the day came when it was time for me and Maria to pack our bags. We travelled up to the Lake District by train and then got a taxi to the hotel. We were both looking forward to time away, on our own together.

We arrived at the hotel during a downpour and strong winds, which made us doubt our decision. But the moment we walked through the doors of the hotel our mood changed. The hotel was delightful – warm and cosy, with welcoming staff. The view from our room was stunning, even on a wet and windy day. Looking out of the window and admiring the view, I remembered that phrase about there being no such thing as bad weather, just inappropriate clothing. Our room was standard but very well presented, with every facility we'd need. By the time we'd checked in and unpacked, it was time for our evening meal. We changed our clothes from casual to smart. Maria looked beautiful, but then she always did. I knew I was truly in love with this woman. When I was with her I felt like the sky was the limit. She gave me a sense of truly believing that I could walk on water. She brought out the best in me, and I hoped that she felt the same.

Our evening meal was wonderful. The staff told us about how the ingredients were sourced locally, and even the chef had been born not too far from the hotel. Once we had finished our meal we went over to the bar, which was very traditional, well kept with a large open fire, which was roaring. It looked and felt so inviting, and we managed to get a table not too far from it. We talked to another young couple who were also staying at the hotel, and after a few minutes they asked if we minded if they joined us, which we didn't. We sat talking for a few hours – they were good company and very interesting. The lady, Nina, was an air stewardess, and Martin was a pilot. They both worked for the same company but very rarely got to be on the same flight, which to me sounded very unfortunate. They told us that they liked their jobs, but their lives felt constantly on the move – so much so they had rented out their home, so when they had time off work they just stayed in hotels in various parts of the UK, mainly beauty spots. And if they had paperwork to do, they'd travel home to Martin's parents' place; they had a big house, so they could live there when needed. They were both working towards owning their own house mortgage-free before they had any children, and that way they hoped Nina could stay at home with the children. Their plan sounded really appealing; both their jobs paid well so their goal looked within reach. Before the evening ended, the four of us planned to go out the next day. Maria and I were so pleased to be in their company; they had many stories to tell.

We returned to our room. Maria was leading the way down the narrow corridor, and I followed close behind. I had a fire burning in my heart that couldn't be contained, and I felt myself getting warmer. Just before we reached our room, Maria paused for a moment, so I stopped too. That's when she turned and looked at me straight, our eyes locking. Then she gave me the most desirable smile, and I felt my knees go weak. I was now in the palm of her hand, and she knew it.

I will spare you the details because a gentleman never tells; however, the next morning we didn't want to leave the bedroom.

By the time we finally got up, we had missed breakfast, and Martin and Nina were waiting for us. The weather was grey and damp, but Martin and Nina were dressed for the occasion, and soon we were too.

Martin and Nina had stayed there many times before, so that was very helpful. They knew of a really good place for lunch; it was a two-mile walk, but that didn't matter as we had nothing else to do that day. We had a really fun day. They were a really interesting couple to listen to – you could say they were flying high – and the conversation flowed all day.

We got back to the hotel much later than we had planned, but it didn't matter because our time with Martin, and Nina was such fun. They weren't dining that evening because they had an early start so needed to call it a day. We exchanged contact details and said our goodbyes. Many times over the years wondered if their plans had worked out for them.

The rest of our stay went well, and when the time came

for us to leave we felt like we needed more time, just us two together. Our relationship had moved on over that weekend – not only were we compatible in life, but also in love. Maria was more than I could've ever asked for.

*

When we got back from the Lake District we both knew and felt that our relationship had become much closer. Maria spent more and more time at my place, and the closer it got to me leaving the more we were inseparable. I asked Maria if she wanted to move into my place while I was away, but she declined. Maria told me that she wouldn't be happy in my place on her own, knowing I wasn't there, and I fully understood. I wasn't going to rent my place out this time after the trouble I had last time. But I was concerned about how long my place was going to be left for. I asked my brothers and sisters if when they were passing they would just check up on the place. They all agreed, and Maria was going to do the same thing.

Khan put on an early Christmas dinner at his place. I thought this a good idea, and I'd already done my Christmas shopping so that everyone would have their presents before I left. It was an unforgettable day.

Just before my departure, Maria and I spent the last two days together, alone. The ten weeks had flown by, and I really didn't want to leave this time. The day finally arrived, and it was very difficult for both me and Maria. I was very grateful to think that my years in the military were coming to an end and that the plumbing course had gone well but still needed to pass the test, so I was leaving that for my return.

I would be gone six months and two weeks, approximately. Late spring would see my return, but this time my leave would only be three weeks, followed by my last call of duty, which was going to be a long stretch – eight months. Once that was done, my years as a soldier would be at an end. I realised I would miss Christmas again. I could have broken those eight months down into two halves, but I just wanted to get it over with. I'd had enough, and now my life was moving in a new direction.

Maria and I had talked about our farewell and had decided we were going to be very grown up about it. We called it a formal departure – straightforward and getting on with the job at hand. We never focused on my leaving, just my returning; that was the best way for us to separate. Maria focused on her journalism and helping Alex, but she wrote to me a lot too. She wrote me some fantastic letters, and because by then she was part of the family I got all their news too, so I felt like I wasn't missing anything. Her letter gave me a clear vision of exactly how things were. I had never had that before I'd met her, and I really enjoyed receiving her letters. I couldn't wait for them to arrive. Between the two of us, we worked our way through our time apart, even though Christmas was hard because it should really have been our first Christmas together. Maria did do FaceTime with the whole family though, which was nice. That year, Alex had invited everyone to his place – there were eighteen in total. Maria said it took a lot of planning and organising, and she was grateful for that because it passed a lot of time and provided a distraction.

Once the winter was over and spring had started to take hold I could start thinking about getting home. While I was gone, Jon managed to rent my place to one of his clients. His company was building a new home – a couple had sold their old house to invest in the new one and they needed a place to live for three months. This was the perfect situation and a great help to me. I could afford the mortgage, but I felt like I was wasting my money because I wasn't living in the house, and it gave me peace of mind knowing that someone was living there. The extra money would come in handy once I started looking for a van too.

At long last, there were only two more weeks to go, so I allowed myself to start planning ahead. There was only one hitch though: Jon's customers' build had run over, and his clients really needed my place for another two months. I was upset about this, but it was my brother, so what could I say? Plus they were really looking after the place this time, so I wasn't going to make a fuss because I was only back for three weeks. Maria suggested I stay over at Alex's estate, but I didn't really want to do that; for some reason, I didn't think that was a good move. I decided to go back to Josephine's – that was the best thing for me at this time. I wasn't too pleased with Jon, to be honest, but there wasn't any point in making a big deal out of it.

*

When I left the barracks, Maria was waiting for me outside. This was also a new experience for me, and a delightful, heartwarming one too. It really felt important, as if I needed to tell everyone that Maria was there. I didn't, of course, but the sense of being wanted by Maria was overwhelming for me. When I first joined up as a youngster, Josephine would wait for me and pick me up, but those days are long gone, so having Maria standing there was an excellent feeling.

Jon had offered me three weeks' work, but I needed a week off, and then I was going to take my plumbing exam, and after that, it would be a case of planning my return. I thanked Jon, but I just wasn't going to be home for long enough.

97

Maria and I spent the next two days together at Maria's place. We didn't do anything too serious, just lunch out and a few late suppers, and of course talking – lots of talking. Maria's place is nice but too small for me; however, it's ideal for Maria. To me, it felt like a doll's house, and in fact, that was just how it looked, even from the outside. The first time I saw it, I thought of a Disney cartoon – I couldn't get over it. I remembered asking Maria if Snow White and the seven dwarves had ever lived there, because when I stood up my head was almost touching the ceiling. Maria laughed and it became a running joke. Maria had a good sense of fun and humour.

The day of my plumbing exam arrived. It felt just like being back at school, only this time I had much more confidence. The exam was fairly straightforward and I passed with flying colours. On the last week of my leave, I did a few tidy-up jobs for Josephine around the house and the shop. Nothing major, just little things that needed to be done; Josephine disliked broken bits and pieces.

My time at home was nearing the end and I needed to focus on getting back on duty. This was my last call and I was truly grateful for that. My relationship with Maria had started to feel very serious and I needed to hold on to it with both hands; everything felt right. After this call of duty, I would have completed fifteen years of service, and I felt very proud of myself. I could've moved up the ranks if I had wanted to, but I was satisfied with what I had gained and achieved. Being in the military had stood me in good stead, and now I was in a good position to leave, and it was the right time.

As I'd done so many times before, I prepared myself mentally for the return to service; I knew it was going to be a hard farewell. Fifteen years is a lifetime, and from the very start that's all I'd intended to do.

As part of our straightforward, matter-of-fact farewell, Maria had left me at Josephine's the night before, which we'd decided was the easiest way to separate because you don't feel like you are properly gone just yet. I was glad I decided to stay with Josephine because it meant we had a nice catch-up, like in the old days.

I got stuck back straight into work, but this time it seemed harder. Maria wrote her letters and we both stayed focused, but the time seemed to be going in slow motion.

Christmas felt lonely – very lonely in fact. That year I seemed to miss everyone more than I had ever done before. I contented myself by daydreaming about the next Christmas, planning and thinking of how to make it the best. Jon did Christmas for everyone at his place. Maria was invited, but that year she had decided to spend it with her friends, knowing that the next year we would spend it together.

After the big day had passed, the next thing was New Year's Eve, which again had never bothered me before, but this year was different, and once again it seemed to drag. The lads always tried to make more of New Year than Christmas, because New Year's Eve, for one reason or another, doesn't seem to be as important as Christmas; it's more like a fun thing.

Once Christmas and New Year were out of the way I could start to look forward to the end of my service, which couldn't come quickly enough. I hadn't said anything to the lads about my release because sometimes it can upset the regiment. I knew this because a few of the lads I became very good friends with told me they were leaving and I remember feeling saddened. So much so that I had felt like leaving myself.

The day finally came, and I got up, packed my bag and signed out. Then I left the barracks for the last time. Surprisingly, I didn't feel upset – it was more of a sense of achievement. I felt very proud of myself. I had served our Queen and Country and in doing so I had learnt so much. I felt as though I was a very strong man, ready to take on the world that stood in front of me. I was entering the next chapter in my life; my priorities had changed the moment I took that first step outside of the barracks.

Maria was my first priority. I knew that I wanted to spend the rest of my life with her. Jon had managed to ensure my house was ready for my return and informed me that he would meet me at my place with the keys. I couldn't wait to get home.

As promised, Jon was there. I was very happy to see him. I have to say that after the last time, I couldn't help but feel slightly anxious as I opened the front door, but there wasn't any need: the customers who had been renting my place were by all accounts quite well to do. Jon told me they loved staying there, and they had even made friends in the village, which I hadn't even done yet.

As I wandered through the house I couldn't believe my eyes. They'd had TVs fitted in both bedrooms, a new carpet in the lounge, and the sofa and curtains had been cleaned. Lastly, they had even put up a lovely garden shed. They had really looked after the place and gone above and beyond to thank me for providing a place to live while they were without a home.

Within twenty minutes of my return, Josephine came round, followed by Maria – she had brought a bottle of wine with her. Jon phoned Fay, who came straight from work, picking up May and Vy on the way. Khan, Linda and the girls arrived in time for tea, which we'd all decided should be a takeaway, and then Alex joined us too. It was an unexpected surprise, and a great way to celebrate and mark the end of my military career.

We had a really nice evening. I have to say I was very overwhelmed and things got a bit emotional for me at times, though I didn't let it show – a force of habit of being in the military.

The night came to an end and finally Maria and I were left alone. I couldn't tell you how pleased I was to be back in her company. We sat on the sofa in total silence, watching the TV for over an hour, just cuddling each other. I couldn't even tell you what we were watching; we were just so happy to be back together.

The next day Maria got up and went straight to work, and I planned to get straight on with sorting out my van and getting all the tools I would need to start up my new business. We both wanted to make the next step, and Maria was going to move in with me the next week. She had already told Alex and had made a start on packing up her things at the cottage. Alex was pleased for us, plus it meant he could rent out the cottage as a holiday let. Maria told him that I thought it was Snow White's cottage, so that's how he was going to market the cottage so it would appeal to young families.

*

The first month seemed to go very quickly. Maria moved in, and I managed to find a van and got my first few jobs. I set up a Facebook page and started to build my profile. Maria had taken on a bit more work for Alex and Tom over at the estate, helping with advertising and social media, but we had both agreed that our working week would finish at 3 pm on Fridays so that Saturday and Sunday were just for us – unless of course there were unforeseen circumstances.

Everything was going to plan. We were both very happy together. Even living at my place seemed to come naturally. There wasn't much we disagreed about, and if we did we just turned into a joke. I think the key to our success was that we were both old enough to know better and understand what is most important. I was thirty-two and Maria was twenty-eight, and that was another big advantage – we had matured. Maria wanted a family and so did I; we had spoken much about this, and it was in both of our thoughts. Everything was moving in the right direction.

Then one day, out of the blue – for no reason that I could think of – the bank called me. I was on a job at the time, and I let it go to voicemail as I think it's very unprofessional to be using the phone while at work. Job done, back in the van I listened to the message: someone called Christine explained that she was from the bank's fraud department, and she needed to speak to me at my earliest convenience. I started to panic, and I phoned straight back.

Christine sounded very nice and assured me that everything was going to be okay so long as I followed her instructions. She asked me if I had used my debit card at any point that day.

I quickly replied no.

Christine then informed me that someone was trying to buy a van with my card.

My heart started racing. I couldn't afford to lose any money; I had only just bought my van, I had the mortgage to think about, plus all the outlay for my tools.

I asked Christine if there was a mistake, because I

myself had only just bought a van two weeks previously.

Christine told me that the card was being debited today for £14,205.

I was in a complete panic. I couldn't lose my money.

Christine assured me that she could stop the transaction, and there was no need to panic. She was very calm and spoke very clearly, and I felt very reassured.

She told me, 'I can see everything that's going on, and I can stop this transaction. All I need is the last three digits of your pin code.'

I'd been using the card a lot recently so I didn't even have to look. I told her the last three digits.

That's when the line went dead.

That's odd, I thought. She was so nice and helpful, and then she hung up on me.

And then it dawned on me. Had I just been scammed? A sick, falling feeling came over me, as if I was plummeting down a deep dark hole. The back of my throat felt dry. I started to sweat.

I fired up the van and went straight to the bank. A member of staff came straight to me – he must have seen the panic on my face. I asked to see my business manager, but she wasn't available.

I felt my legs go weak.

'Is it something I can help with?' the young clerk asked.

'I really hope so,' I said.

He took my details and logged into my account. After a moment, he confirmed that the transaction for £14,205 had gone through.

'Can't you stop it?' I asked.

Before the clerk could reply, I ran out of the bank and started to vomit, and I couldn't stop myself.

What had I done? I felt so foolish. Stomach finally

empty, I sat on the stone steps of the bank and replayed everything over and over in my head. Christine had sounded so nice and reassuring. She'd said she was from the bank. She was so believable.

I went back inside, and the clerk was waiting for me, with a bottle of water.

'Thanks,' I said shakily as I took it. 'Is there a Christine that works here?' In my heart, I knew the answer was going to be no, but I needed the clerk to confirm it.

I grabbed my phone to bring up the recent calls. I showed the clerk the number that had phoned me. 'She told me that she was part of this branch,' I explained.

'Don't tell me – the fraud team?'

I was stunned. 'Yes – that's what she told me. She was from the fraud team.'

The clerk said, 'I'm really sorry. You're not the first person this has happened to. Let me take your details and I will make arrangements for you to see your business manager as soon as possible. What type of card did you use?'

'Visa debit.'

The clerk winced. 'Visa debit doesn't have the same protections as a credit card, but we might be able to do something. Will you be able to come back tomorrow at 10 am?'

I left the bank, not really wanting to return home. What was I going to tell Maria? More to the point, *how* was I going to tell Maria? I felt so desperate.

I phoned Khan to see if he was at home. He was still at work but would be home within two hours. He asked what was wrong, but I couldn't tell him over the phone.

What to do? I couldn't go to Aunt Josephine's, not until I had spoken to Khan. I occupied myself by tidying the back of my van and cleaning up all my tools. That took an hour, after which I messaged Maria to let her know that I was just heading over to Khan's place before I came home.

When I arrived, Linda and the girls were home. Linda made me a cup of tea and asked me if I wanted anything to eat, but I didn't feel like eating anything. Thankfully Indiana and Nevada were very pleased to see me, and they were the distraction I needed to calm myself down. I made a fuss of them, and just for a brief moment I forgot about my problem.

Then Khan got home. I didn't want to mention the problem in front of the girls, so I asked Khan if I could borrow some of his tools. Once we were inside the shed I told him what had happened.

Khan was upset, and very angry. He asked me for all the details, and once I'd told him he advised me not to say anything to anybody until after I had visited the bank.

From there I went straight home, and much to my relief Maria wasn't home yet. I sat for a while and gathered my thoughts, then I decided to try to push my worries to the back of my mind until the next day. I really didn't want Maria to know. I just hoped I could sort this mess out without Maria ever knowing.

The next day I got up earlier than normal and went for a 10k run. I couldn't sleep anyway, and the run helped clear my mind. When I returned, Maria was just getting up. I made breakfast for us, then Maria left for work, and I showered. The meeting at the bank was 10 am, so I phoned the job I had on for that day and told them I was going to be late.

I arrived at the bank and Beverly, my business manager, was waiting for me. She greeted me with a handshake and a sympathetic smile. We went into a side room and sat down. She asked if I wanted coffee, but I couldn't eat or drink anything at that point; I was still feeling sick.

We went over all the details again. I told Beverly that the woman had assured me she was from the bank's fraud team and working within this branch. Beverly was very nice and when she replied she choose her words very carefully. 'The bottom line was that the bank's systems were secure, and if you give your details, that's something which any court would see as your fault.'

The biggest problem was that I had given the fraudsters the last three digits of my banking pin code. Apparently, the bank would never ask for such details. Beverly looked up the details of the transaction and told me I would need to report the fraud to the police. Beverly then arranged for me a £5,000 overdraft on my business account and advised me to only use the overdraft in an emergency, because the interest rate was very high – 35% to be precise.

This sounded like trouble, but there wasn't any way around it: I needed that overdraft to pay my bills. The problem was I'd never needed to deal with the financial side of things, what with being in the army, so this was all new to me. Until then, all I knew was I worked and the money went into the bank once a month. I was planning on getting an accountant once the business had made its first £5,000.

Beverly picked up the transaction print-out from the printer and paused, before saying that they didn't seem to include any traceable information – not that she could see, anyway. To me, it hardly seemed worth going to the police with such little evidence, but I needed to do this, for not just my benefit but for the benefit of the bank and other customers.

Once I left the bank, I went straight to the police station. That took another hour, and all I got was a crime number.

The bank had made no promises that I would ever get my money back. It was surreal; I felt like I was watching someone else's nightmare, and if I chose, I would be able to step out of the situation. Except this was my life. Facing up to what had happened was very hard, because I felt so foolish. The scam felt like it was too easy to have taken place.

After the police station, I walked down the street to the coffee shop. I sat for a while and wondered how I was going to tell Maria. Aunt Josephine didn't need to know, but Maria did.

Once I got to the job, I focused on my work and that helped clear my head. The job went well, and the guy I was working for was very pleased. He asked me if I had much work on, because he had another job for me, and whether I was interested in doing any more work beyond that.

I told him yes – once I'd been paid for this job, I would take a look at the next one.

The guy was taken aback by what I had said – I could see the look on his face.

I told him, 'Look, mate, I'm sorry for my abrupt attitude, but yesterday I got ripped off for just over fourteen thousand pounds.'

The guy's expression quickly changed. 'I'm so sorry to hear that.' He paused, taking in what I'd just told him. 'Send over your invoice and your bank details, and I'll make sure the money is in your bank tomorrow.'

I shook his hand. 'That would be much appreciated. Thank you.'

He then said, 'Once you've checked your bank account

tomorrow and it's cleared, give me a call if you're interested in any more work.' I turned to go before he added, 'If you don't mind me asking, how the hell have you lost just over fourteen thousand pounds?'

'It was a debit card scam over the phone.'

By the time I'd finished telling him, the guy looked very grave.

'To be honest, I feel like a complete fool,' I said, in conclusion.

'It could happen to anybody. Don't let it bring you down – I know it's easy for me to say that, of course, but if you have any chance of getting the money back, you need the put all your attention into it.'

'You're right,' I replied.

'Have you reported it to the police?'

'Yes, they gave me a crime number and said there isn't anything else they can do at this time.'

The guy rolled his eyes. 'What a joke. And these lowlife scammers know the police can't do much about it. Sometimes I think you're better off not bothering with the police at all.'

'Yes, too right,' I replied, because I'd actually felt worse since dealing with the police.

He reached into his pocket and gave me a business card. 'Your name's Sean – is that right? I'm Karl. It's good to talk to you. I hope you get some luck, and hopefully, I will see you tomorrow.'

'Yes, I'll sort the invoice when I get home.' I said. 'But I can't promise anything for tomorrow because I need to sort out my finances.'

'Understandable. No worries. You've got my card, so as soon as you are sorted give me a call.'

*

Once I got home, I decided that I was going to tell Maria as soon as she got home. How nice that sounded: *when Maria comes home*. Yes, in the last few weeks, this had become Maria's home too, and we were living very comfortably together in my place. Actually, that sounded arrogant – I thought it best to call it our place from now on – yes, that sounded much better. Our place.

I loved Maria more than I could have ever imagined. We were very happy together, and I could say that with confidence. I wished I didn't have to tell her this dreadful news. If I could have just gone and gotten the money back, I would have. But I couldn't. I didn't know who had my money or where it had gone. I remembered Aunt Josephine's words about honesty always being the best policy. 'It's a much cleaner environment,' she said. 'Lies are only dust and dirt.'

After what seemed a lifetime Maria walked in. She looked so happy, and straight away she was chatting about her work, without a care in the world.

Soon she noticed how still and quiet I was and sat down next to me. 'What's the matter?' she said gently.

'I'm okay, but I have something I need to tell you.'

Maria listened and took it all in. She was shocked at first, and then angry. I was afraid of what she'd think of me, but she was supportive, which in all honesty is all I wanted. I knew I wasn't going to get that money back any time soon, if at all.

That night, Maria and I went over my finances until 2 am, but whichever way we looked at it, it wasn't looking good. I had saved enough to last me six months without working – but then the scammers had swooped in and stolen that safety net. The good news was that I'd already started working, but the bad news was that I had repayments on the van, which I hadn't factored into the savings. What with the mortgage and the van, I needed to clear £2,100 per month, which was much more than I'd realised – in fact it was £600 more.

Maria offered to help with the mortgage, but that wasn't what I wanted. Our idea was to save Maria's money for the future. The consequences of the scam were sinking in deeper and deeper as time went on. I was in a mess and it wasn't going to be easy to get out of.

Maria and I decided we would do our best and work through the mess. No matter what, we agreed, we would still enjoy our time together as best we could. But I battled with shame, and told Maria that I was really sorry, and if she wanted to go back home I would fully understand.

Maria said, 'Sean, our journey together has only just started, and I'm not getting off now. I have no intentions of going home.' I was grateful to know she was standing by me.

I knew I needed to work all the hours possible – including weekends, when the pay was better – so our cosy little set-up had been stolen. I asked Maria not to mention anything to Alex because I didn't want Josephine to find out.

Maria nodded firmly. 'This is our problem, and we'll sort it out together.' I loved that Maria had a way of making me feel strong and empowered.

Maria asked if I had mentioned it to any other family members.

'Just Khan, because if Josephine finds out, he will know just how to handle the situation so that Josephine doesn't get stressed.'

Maria frowned. 'What do you think Josephine would do if she was to find out?

'She'll go straight to the bank and put the missing money back into my account.'

'Really?' Maria was wide-eyed. 'Is that what she would do?

'Yep. That's Josephine.'

Maria gazed at me, so I spoke my thoughts out loud.

'I've been very lucky to have been brought up with my brothers and sisters. Aunt Josephine didn't want to take me on at first, and who can blame her, after what my father did? So, I've always been grateful for the life I've had. My family has been brilliant. As a child I never felt any different to Khan, Jon, May and Vy. It wasn't until Khan told me that I actually knew how I came into the world. My mother is a gold-digger and my father is a complete idiot. So I know for sure if Aunt Josephine hadn't taken me on, my life would have been very tough.'

Maria nodded, listening intently.

I continued, 'So I only want to impress her. She was a very good teacher, and I wouldn't want to let her down. I know Josephine will be devastated if she finds out. She'll want to fix things by giving me the money – that's why I don't want her to know.'

Maria reached out and touched my shoulder. 'We will try and work this out.'

I looked straight back at Maria and said, 'Thank you.'

The weeks passed, and I heard nothing from the police or the bank. I had been back to the bank several times and felt like I was just wasting my time, so after about six months I stopped asking questions and just focused on earning as much as I could.

Maria was still working at the paper. She hadn't said anything, but I'd noticed she was also putting more hours in.

I'd hit my overdraft, so my debt was piling up. The bank

had advised me to try not to use the overdraft, but there was no way around it; I couldn't pay my bills without adding £300 to £350 a month to the overdraft, which was fast running out.

I really needed that money I'd lost. That was the starter I needed. I knew if we didn't get on top of this, I could lose the van. I felt like I was on the helter-skelter, going down very fast.

*

The day came when I needed to let the van go. At that point, it was the best thing for us, as it meant I wouldn't need to pay the repayments, or the insurance. And I wasn't self-employed any more – I had a job. Looking back, maybe that was how I should have started.

I didn't know which way to turn for the best. Maria and I were still trying to make the best of our situation. We'd spend our free time over at the estate, which to be honest was like a breath of fresh air. Once we got to the estate, we could switch off. But once we returned to our place it started to feel like returning to the grindstone. We both tried our best, but with no savings, it was very difficult. Without the van that did make things much easier. However, by then it wasn't enough. We considered going to a private lender, but their interest rates were much more than we could've ever paid back. Our biggest problem was that I wasn't bringing in enough money, to pay for our lifestyle. Maybe I should have rented a property and not bought one.

After twelve months the mounting debt was out of control. Khan and Jon – who Khan had told – had visited many times by then with offers of help, but that idea wasn't for me. I loved my independence, and whatever the cost, I planned to keep it.

We never told anyone else about our debts.

Then one day out of the blue I got a letter from the bank asking me if I would like to increase my overdraft, which came as a relief because I didn't realise that was an option for me. I phoned them and increased it to £10,000, which would give me at least another eight months if I was very careful. That gave me hope.

But then I lost my job because the company I was working for was relocating to London. This was a massive blow for us. I really didn't know how to tell Maria, but I did, and as always she tried to look for something positive out of the situation.

But Maria's kindness didn't help with the fact that this wasn't what I'd planned, what I'd given fifteen years' service and hard work for. The worst part was it didn't even feel like I'd been there. My years of service felt like they no longer belonged to me, taken from me by some lowlife. I'd lost my savings and my van, and if I didn't find another job soon, our house would be next.

Maria didn't say anything to me, but while we were over at the estate one Sunday, Tom let it slip that she had asked if her old cottage could be made available.

Tom saw my face. 'Sorry. I shouldn't have said anything, Maria asked me not to mention it to you.'

'Don't worry, Tom. I'm not offended. I don't blame Maria. She's right to ask. At the rate we're going, if I don't get another job we'll be lucky to have a roof over our heads for another six months.'

'Maybe I shouldn't say this,' Tom said, 'but Maria has told me about the situation.'

I looked at Tom and felt completely devastated – not because he knew, but because I hated myself for being such an easy target for the scammers. The mental strain of the scam was almost unbearable.

I told Tom, 'Maria has got to tell someone. I just don't want Josephine to find out.'

'I haven't mentioned it to my father,' Tom said. 'And with regards to the cottage, because it's within the walls of the estate we have only been letting it on a weekly basis – holiday lets, that sort of thing, so if you need the cottage just give me a week's notice. That's all, I need.'

'Thank you. Hopefully we'll be fine, but it's nice to know we have a safety net.'

Tom didn't take the conversation any further, and for that I was grateful.

When we got home I didn't mention to Maria what Tom said. In all honesty, I was grateful to Maria for thinking ahead. Our situation was getting worse by the week. I had been to the bank several times and I didn't feel confident about getting my money back. They assured me they were doing everything possible. It is my belief that they did bear some of the responsibility, because how would the scammers have had my contact number, and how would they know I had that amount in the bank without some inside information? I'd told the bank my theory, and their reply was that they were just opportunistic thieves, but it didn't feel like that to me.

Our next blow was just around the corner though.

Chapter Seven

❦

Maria's newspaper ceased trading. She was devastated. She loved her job and worked very hard for the paper – it was her passion. She loved rooting out the stories, bringing the unknown to light, finding new people and giving them a voice. Without bias, Maria had the natural ability to receive people's stories because everyone trusted her to write the truth, no fabrications. Maria would always try to find the positive in any story and focus on that instead of trying to make things look a lot worse than they were.

Maria was shocked because the bosses didn't tell the staff. Maria knew where they lived, so she and one of her colleagues went to see if they could get any information because obviously they wanted to know about redundancy pay. But there was some more bad news to come: apparently, the paper had been in financial difficulties for some time, and the receiver had gone in, so there wasn't going to be any redundancy pay. The offices were rented, and the rent was in arrears. It was a bigger mess than I was in. But I didn't know about all this immediately. After Maria returned from seeing her bosses she was very quiet. I could see she was angry about something, but she wouldn't tell me what.

She didn't say much at all to me that day, but a few days after she'd absorbed all the information, she filled me in. I wasn't worried about the newspaper; my only concern was for Maria. She was truly devastated. She hadn't seen this coming. I felt terrible because I had no way of consoling her – what did I have to offer now? I'd lost my van, lost my job, and in all honesty, I was going to lose my house very soon. I felt so defeated. After fifteen years' service to my country, I was trained to be a fighter, to be tough, and to be able to handle any situation under immense pressure. But none of that could have prepared me for the mess I was now living in. I wanted to reassure Maria that everything was going to be okay, but I couldn't even do that. Inside I was a broken man. I did my best not to let anybody else see what I was feeling. I needed to be as strong as possible, and that is very hard with a ten-tonne weight resting on your shoulders. I kept my devastation to myself.

The next day I went to see Khan because I needed to tell Aunt Josephine before anybody else did. I had started to wish I had told her sooner, but I never thought it would come to this. Khan listened, then phoned Jon to come straight round. My brothers told me that they would do everything possible to help. I thanked them and told them I already knew that, but my concern was Josephine – the last thing I wanted to do was let her down.

'Josephine brought me up to the best of her ability, and look at the mess I'm in,' I said. 'I consider myself very lucky to be part of this family. I know that Josephine will try and find a way to blame herself. She gave me a very good start in life, and I shouldn't be in this mess.'

Khan replied, 'Mother is tougher than you might think.'

Jon went on to say, 'But there isn't any need to tell her anything, because we are going to help you out of this problem.'

I shook my head and said, 'No you're not. This is my mess, and I'll sort it out myself.'

'And how do you intend to do that?' asked Jon.

I threw my hands up in a shrug. 'I'm not sure at this moment, but you saved my life once before. This time I'm going to save myself.'

Khan and Jon said nothing, just shook their heads in frustration.

'Look,' I continued, 'don't think for one minute I don't appreciate you offering to get me out of this mess. I sincerely do appreciate your offer of help, but as a man I feel totally defeated, and I didn't do fifteen years' service only to come out and fail in life – that's just not how it was supposed to be. No – I will figure out a way through this, that's what my heart's telling me to do.'

'And what about Maria?' Khan asked.

'When this all first started, we were in it together, but she's just lost her job. She's taken it very hard, and if she wanted to go back home I wouldn't blame her, or hold it against her. I love her too much for that.'

'Listen, Sean. Why don't you come with me, and we'll tell Mother together?'

'I do think that would be best if you don't mind,' I sighed.

We left it there, and Jon took me back to our place. Our place – I didn't even feel safe saying that any more. I loved our place. Back at the start, I was so happy, knowing I had that security, all my years of hard work had been worth it. I wasn't looking forward to telling Josephine, but it was a job that needed to be done.

*

On Wednesday, Khan finished work and picked me up. We drove to the shop because it was Wednesday, which is when Josephine puts in a few extra hours tidying up the shop and catching up on paperwork. As we walked into the shop, Josephine looked at us slightly surprised, but at the same time she was very pleased to see us.

'Boys! I'm glad you're here. You're just in time,' she smiled.

Khan looked at me, shook his head, smiled and said, 'Some things will never change.'

Josephine had been moving the stock from the back storage room to the front, so we helped her out, and then once we'd done that, we cleaned the stock room. Josephine had us washing the walls and everything – it was a full-on spring clean. For a few hours, I felt better than I'd done in ages. My problems faded to the back of my mind.

The stock room was spotless by the time we'd finished.

'Well, that couldn't have been better timing,' Josephine said as she put the kettle on. 'I wouldn't have got all that done tonight.'

We sat down with our cups of tea, and then Josephine said, 'So, what's brought you two here on this beautiful evening?'

I didn't hesitate. I spoke up. 'It's me.'

Josephine looked straight at me, and her face had gone very pale already.

'I'm okay – it's not my health,' I began.

'Is Maria expecting a baby?' Josephine blurted out.

I smiled, thinking how nice that would be if that was my reason for this visit. But then that sentence made me feel cold, because as much as I wanted children of my own, this wasn't the time.

'No, nothing like that. I've got into some financial difficulties.'

There. I'd said it. I felt a sense of relief at that moment. How much Josephine wanted to know about this situation was now down to her, because without question I wasn't saying anything else.

Josephine sat in silence for a few seconds and then asked, 'How much financial difficulty?'

I breathed in and held it for a moment. 'Quite a substantial amount.'

I kept my eyes on the ground while the next question came. 'Are the financial difficulties your fault?'

Thankfully Khan stepped in. 'No, Mother. Sean has been the victim of scammers.'

Josephine went quiet for a few minutes. The silence was deafening, like someone was screaming in my ear. Then she looked at us both and said, 'Is there anything we can do to put this situation right?'

Khan spoke up again. 'Me and Jon have been offering help, but Sean won't accept our offer.'

Josephine's expression changed. She looked at me and asked, 'Why won't you accept help?'

'Because I feel totally defeated, and I haven't spent fifteen years in the military to be ruined by some lowlife scammers. I'm determined to sort this situation out myself. I'm prepared to do whatever that takes.'

Josephine said, 'I hope you're not going to lose your home.'

Again I felt cold and empty. Josephine wasn't going to like the response. I looked straight at her and said, 'I sincerely wish I could sing you a better song, but there isn't one available at the minute. The answer to your question? Yes, I'm going to lose my home within the next month.'

The look on Josephine's face was unbearable. She looked at Khan and said, 'Can we put this right?'

Khan said, 'Yes we can, but the problem we have is Sean. He won't accept any help. Both me and Jon have spent weeks offering help.'

Josephine looked at me sternly. It made me feel like a child again, like I had just pulled over her favourite vase and smashed it on the floor.

'Why will you not accept help from your brothers, Sean?' she said sharply.

'Because it's my mess, and I'm going to get out of it myself. You've all given me more than enough. Khan and Jon have got their own lives to pay for, and I'm not allowing myself to infringe on their lives.'

Josephine was in deep thought, then she said, 'What about if I help you?' Before I could say anything she added, 'I still have plenty of money left over from the sale of our family home.'

I smiled at Josephine and said, 'You've done more than enough for me, and I'm not allowing you or any of the family to do anything else. I'm old enough to take care of myself now.'

Josephine's face softened into a look of sorrow. She looked at Khan, then back to me and said, 'Sean, you are the baby of our family, and we all only want the best for you.'

I looked at them both and told them, 'I know that, and I am well aware that you will all do everything in your power to help me. But you have all taught me well, and I'm going to get out of this mess myself. The only reason I can do that is I have your strength behind me.'

Josephine looked at me and said, 'I know I didn't give birth to you, but I can see myself in you. When I was young, I had your determination, but if I'm totally honest I wish I had not been so hard on myself. When your father left me, my brother offered many times to help me, but like you, I was determined to fight the battle on my own. That way, every small victory was mine to enjoy. So don't think for one minute I don't understand what it's like to be in your shoes, because I do. And knowing all this doesn't make it easy for me to stand and watch. So I'm going to allow you to do whatever it is you're going to do, because the truth is I know I can't stop you. But you need to promise me, here and now, in front of Khan, that if things get too hard for you, you will let us help you.'

Eyes on the ground, I nodded my head. 'Yes. I promise.'

As I raised my head, Josephine was looking straight at me, and she had tears in her eyes. 'Sean,' she said, 'No matter what happens, we are all very proud of you.'

We walked Josephine back to her place, then Khan dropped me back home.

'Thanks for supporting me like that. I couldn't have broken that news to Mother on my own. It would have been too hard.'

Khan looked at me, gave me a hug and said, 'My offer will always be on the table.'

Now that Aunt Josephine knew of my situation, it felt like my problem was more real. I'd really hoped I would be able to get through it without telling her.

*

My next task was to contact social services because within the next month I would be homeless, and I was hoping that if I made contact sooner I could avoid the streets. At that point, I had no idea what was to come.

Maria wanted us to move back into her old cottage on the estate, but that wasn't for me. I had just turned down all the help I could ever wish for from my own family, and I wasn't going to let anybody else help me. I told Maria that if she wanted to move back there until we got sorted, I wouldn't mind. But she didn't want to move back without me.

I knew Alex wasn't pleased about this situation because he phoned me and told me there wasn't any need to struggle when it came to finding a place to live when he had the estate. In fact, I could tell that he was very angry with me, and he thought I should have more consideration for Maria.

I knew in my heart Alex was right, but I had my pride and a sense of self-motivation, a drive within me – that was going to help put right the mistakes that I had made. And nothing and nobody was going to change my mind, even if that meant Maria moving back home. I was not taking this lying down. I would not be defeated, not after fifteen years' service. It was too much to bear.

Sometimes I had the feeling that this problem happened to me for a reason. I had some kind of burning ambition. The reason was unclear but I needed to work my way through this situation, that I knew for sure.

After a few days of thinking about my next move, I decided to pay a visit to social services. I didn't really know why, but I was dreading it. I got myself dressed, tidily in a shirt, tie, and my best coat. When I arrived, it was nothing like how I'd imagined it: the place was very welcoming and had a pleasant feel to it. Although there wasn't anything pleasant about me being there, I didn't feel in any way patronised – in fact after my visit I felt massive relief. They took all my details so that I was in the system, and they gave me the details of various charities for ex-military. They informed me that they would be in touch within the next twenty-one working days, which did seem like a long time, but I'm not moaning because I needed help, and I was grateful for anything.

Maria wouldn't come with me because she wasn't prepared to accept that kind of help. She felt that she didn't need it. I fully understood her reasons because she had the cottage, and for her, she said anything else felt selfish. But for me it was different. I needed help but wanted to maintain my independence and not rely on my family completely. I promised her that I would do everything in my power to put us back where we were. Maria knew I meant that.

We started to pack up the house. I decided to sell most of my stuff. What was the point in keeping it when I didn't know how long I would be in this situation? Besides, when I got another place I might not like what I had before. It may well remind me of a past that I would prefer to forget.

*

A few days later, I had a meeting with the bank to sort out my finances, accompanied by a good solicitor that Jon got for me. After several hours, it was decided that the bank would take the house and in return, they would clear all my debt, including the overdraft. They didn't really want to clear the overdraft, but the solicitor gave them no choice – it was that or a court case, because according to the solicitor they shouldn't have given me the overdraft in the first place as they knew full well that I was in serious trouble after being scammed. The solicitor also advised them that he and his firm would look into the scams to see if they could find any connection to the bank. The bank didn't like this, and the branch manager told the solicitor that he was twisting the bank's arm, and that was against the law. But I came out much better than I thought. I lost my 20K deposit, but my overdraft was almost 10K, so it didn't feel so bad. It was the solicitor that won the day. He did cost me £350 plus VAT, but he saved me much more. Jon is always ahead of the game.

I actually refused Jon's offer of a solicitor, but he wasn't taking no for an answer. He told me he wanted to be there for moral support, and I agreed. Then he told the solicitor the time and date, and when I got there the solicitor was waiting for me, and I didn't have the heart to turn him away. Jon is the clever one, that's for sure. I wish I had his intelligence.

I sold most of the stuff so I only had my clothes and kitchen accessories – knives, forks, plates, pots and pans, that sort of thing. Maria took those things and anything else that was left to the estate, where Alex had a lock-up container with space available. The day came when it was time to vacate the house, and I didn't hang about; I made arrangements for them to collect the keys at 8 am. They also brought along a locksmith to change the door locks; I don't know why, but that was the part that got to me the most. I remembered thinking to myself, why change the locks? They were perfectly good locks. It meant that our place was no longer our place. I tried to just walk away, but this was much harder than I'd thought. It was getting on top of me, and my anger started to rise. I knew I needed to suppress this emotion because I needed all my energy for the road ahead, but I couldn't help it – I felt anger, disappointment, embarrassment, and anxiety. I was thankful that Maria wasn't around; she'd left the day before. This was just about the worst thing that had happened to me.

I started to wish I had taken the help that Jon and Khan had offered me in the beginning; where was my brain?! Then a thought entered my head: I'm a soldier and I've seen some pretty tough stuff. I've been put down before and I've always managed to get back up. And for some reason, I remembered Captain Tom, the elderly guy who raised millions by walking around his garden, and I remembered what he said: 'Tomorrow will be a better day.' I smiled to myself and walked away. And I never looked back. Tomorrow will be a better day.

The guy from the bank who collected the keys didn't seem to be in the least bit bothered about the job – water off a duck's back. After all, the banks will do anything to raise money, because that's their game – MONEY. I don't hold it against them, I'm just glad that's not my job.

Maria and I decided it was best if she stayed home for the next few weeks until I sorted myself out. I had another appointment with social services because they hadn't managed to arrange anything so far, so by then, I was an emergency case. My usual caseworker wasn't there that day, and instead, I was seen by Nova, whose name reminded me of a hotel. Nova had no info on my case whatsoever because Frank, who was dealing with me, had locked my file and no one could get in. They tried to contact Frank, but he was in the Dominican Republic and with the time difference and poor signal they couldn't make contact. Just my luck.

After a few hours of hanging about, they decided I would need to spend a few days in a local hotel. They informed me they take so many rooms in this hotel for people in my position. I asked how long I would be there, and they replied that they hoped to have me out of there within a couple of weeks.

The hotel was within walking distance, so I made my way over. When I arrived I realised had seen this building many times before and had never taken any notice. It didn't look like a hotel; it was more like a halfway house.

There was security at the entrance, and that's when I knew it was definitely no hotel. The security guy stopped me, asked me a few details, checked his records, and then let me in; he was nice enough. Then I walked up to a reception area which looked more like a control office. There were ten CCTV monitors with someone sitting watching the screens. Another guy was sorting out the admin, and the whole reception area was behind thick glass. I started to feel very uneasy.

The admin guy asked me my name and then told me, 'You're in room five, on the third floor.' He gave me a key and told me that if I lost the key I would have to pay for it, and if I damaged anything in the room – TV, kettle etc – I would also have to pay for that. I took a deep breath and told him, 'Okay.'

He looked at me and said, 'Sorry, it's just the way it is here.'

'No worries,' I replied, but inside I didn't feel like I had no worries. I looked at the key. It had a big wooden tag attached to it. This wasn't what I had in mind, but then I reminded myself that this was my choice, so I had to get on with it.

I made my way over to the lift, which I then saw was out of order. I only had one bag to carry up the stairs, thankfully. I got to my room, expecting the worst – but thankfully as I opened the door a clean smell greeted me, and I felt grateful. The room was only small, but it was clean. The bed was only a single; I pulled back the bedding and that was also nice and fresh. At least I should be able to get a good night's sleep. The next thing I looked for was the kettle and then the TV – neither was broken, and both worked. There was one wardrobe and a small window. It wasn't great in any way, shape or form, but I had a roof over my head, and on this damp miserable day I was grateful. I settled myself in as best I could. I had work in the morning, so I wasn't planning on being up too late. I phoned Maria, and she had some good news: she had managed to get another job with a local magazine. Maria was delighted; this was good news. I got to bed at about ten and went straight to sleep.

At about 1 am it was as if everybody in the building had decided to get up. The doors were being slammed and people were arguing and shouting. This went on until around 7 am. I left for work at 7.30 am, and the security guards were outside my room, trying to calm down the situation, whatever that was. I didn't hang around to find out. As I walked away from the building, the police drove past. I didn't think about this too much.

I had a job on a small building site; it was a new-build office block. While walking to work I started to think about Maria and her new job, which didn't start until the next month.

My day didn't go too badly, and on the way home I stopped off for something to eat. I only had a microwave in the room for cooking, and that type of cooking wasn't for me. I got back to my hotel, which felt more like a hostel, and it was as if everybody had abandoned the place – it was as dead as a doornail, quite a contrast to when I left this morning.

I got to my room, had a quick shower, put the TV on and fell fast asleep. I slept until around 2 am, when the hotel came back to life again – doors slamming, people shouting, what sounded like rioting. This went on all night; I didn't get any more sleep. I left at 7 am, the police were outside. The penny dropped: this hostel was full of drug addicts. That's why they were up all night and kicking off.

As I was leaving I spoke to one of the police officers and asked, 'Are you here every day?'

He glanced at me. 'Are you new to this place?'

I confirmed that I was, but the officer wasn't up for a chat, so I kept walking. Seeing the police reminded me of that night in the pub. Then a thought entered my head: no wonder the police weren't that interested in the incident in the pub after they realised nobody was hurt. Dealing with that place must be a big drain on them and their resources.

The working day felt long and hard because I was so tired, and I was glad when it was home time. Before I got back to the hostel I spoke to Maria, and we made our arrangements for the weekend. Maria wanted to visit me, and I made all excuses I could think of. I didn't want her to visit me in the hostel. I preferred her not to see what was going on there. I got back to the room and fell asleep right away – until around midnight, when it all kicked off again. I didn't leave my room, but I knew that the place was full of drug addicts, and being amongst these addicts was very dangerous. I'd seen stuff in the paper. I left for work at 6.30 am the next morning, hoping I could start work early so I could get finished early too.

When I arrived at the building site I went and saw the site manager and explained my situation and asked if I could start earlier and finish earlier, and that way I could fit in with the addicts.

He nodded sympathetically. 'Leave it with me and I'll try and sort something out for you.'

I only had one more weekday left, and then I was staying over at Maria's for the weekend. I finished my work and called in at the pub for a pint and something to eat. I made it last as long as possible as I was dreading returning to the hostel. I made up my mind that I wasn't staying there one more minute than I needed to; my stay would be as short as possible. That night it was the exact same routine.

Saturday morning I got up and went to the laundrette and did my washing ready for the coming week. I went back to the hostel, put my room tidy and left. I spent Saturday and Sunday with Maria at her place. We had a nice couple of days together. Alex was very annoyed with me and he made his feelings clear, but I knew that he was only concerned. I listened respectfully to him, but I knew that this was something I had to go through, and I wasn't changing my mind. Maria was very supportive of me though, and that was all that mattered to me then. Truth be told, I couldn't do this if I thought I was going to lose her. Maria was my drive, and I wanted to save as much of my money as possible so that I could get us back on track. By using the hostel I was saving on living costs, and Maria was also saving by being back at home. Maria was helping her father three days a week to cover the cost of her being in the cottage. But if I moved in I would feel obliged to help out too, and I'd prefer to keep my job.

On Monday morning Maria dropped me back at work.

The site manager found me and said, 'I've spoken to my supervisor and he gave me permission to get you a key cut so you can start at 4 am, to help you out while you're living in the hostel.'

I felt so grateful. That meant I could get more rest while the drug addicts and alcoholics were quiet.

*

After work, I did my usual routine of stopping off at the pub for something to eat, and then back to the hostel, but when I arrived, security was waiting for me.

'Sean, before you go to your room, I need to tell you something.'

From the look on his face, I thought someone had died.

'Your room got broken into while you were away. We tried to phone you, but there was no answer. We've tidied up and had the locksmith in to change the lock.' We also needed to phone the police and report the crime, so whatever is missing you will be able to claim from our insurance.'

I wasn't best pleased, but I wasn't surprised either. I knew full well there wasn't anything of any value in my room. All my good stuff was with Maria. The security guard walked with me to the room. When I opened the door, the room looked okay; the kettle was gone, and my clothes were all thrown around, but that was it. I was glad I hadn't brought anything of value with me. I'd wanted to keep my stuff to a minimum, in the hopes that I was only passing through and not staying for dinner. The security guard apologised, adding that it happens all the time. 'The drug addicts make running this place hard work at times. We have to offer them accommodation for so long and then the funding will stop once social services realise that they will not look for or go to work. The addicts are not all the same though. We've seen some of them completely turn their lives around, and the best bit about it is that some of them go on to help others get out of the vicious circle. Because an ex-addict understands better than anyone else just how hard it is to kick the habit. But then you also have the addict whose life has been so crap that they find it hard to deal with it, and they can never find their way off drugs.'

'What happens once they leave here?' I wondered out loud.

'They go back to the streets. They all get one shot at rehabilitation but for many, one's just not enough. The lucky ones will get a second chance, but they work hard to get that, and it's the same with alcohol. In my experience, there isn't any difference between drugs and alcohol. They both ruin lives.' The security guard shook his head, coming back to the present moment. 'Anyway, I'd better let you sort yourself out. Here's your new key. Do you want me to take the old one?'

'Yes, please. Thanks.'

The guard took his leave and I locked the door, picked up my clothes and packed them away. Then I put the TV on and fell asleep – it was the same routine as last week, but this week I could get up at 3 am and be gone by 3.30 am. Just like clockwork, it all kicked off about midnight, and by 2 am it sounded like they were having an all-out war. As I went to leave at 3.30 am, I opened my door and what I saw was horrifying: a woman was holding a knife to the throat of a young lad, who didn't look much older than twelve.

As my door shut behind me, they both looked at me. I could see the young lad was very scared.

This wasn't something I could just walk away from. 'What's going on here?' I asked.

'Mind your own fucking business if you know what's good for you,' she replied.

'Let the young lad go. I'm sure he doesn't deserve this,' I reasoned.

The woman looked at me. She seemed to be in a raging temper, her red sweaty face glowing. 'He's been ripping me off, stealing my drugs.'

'I haven't stolen anything!' the young lad whimpered. He tried to turn his head to look at me, but as he did so the

131

woman pressed hard on the knife, and I watched as the skin of his neck opened up.

I froze for a second, but then I was in motion. I raced forward to help the boy, and the woman must have thought I was going for her, so she turned the knife on me. I didn't realise anything was wrong at first, because I was only thinking about the young lad, who by then was lying on the floor, blood pumping out of his neck. I shouted for help and a man came running towards me and then a woman. I pressed my hand on the young lad's neck to try and stop the blood, but it was almost impossible. Security phoned for an ambulance, and I kept talking to the young lad so that he didn't lose consciousness.

The ambulance arrived very quickly and the paramedics took over. As I stood up it became very clear that I had also been stabbed. The paramedics phoned for another ambulance, and then the police arrived. Thankfully my injury was only minor but I still needed to go to the hospital to be stitched up. I needed tests just in case the knife was dirty. Thankfully, the young lad survived, but only just about. The doctors informed me that if I hadn't been there he would have died, no question. I felt sick with shock over the whole experience.

Chapter Eight

❧

I got out of the hospital about 3 pm that day and was advised to rest until the stitches had been removed to avoid any unnecessary further injury. I took a taxi and went straight to my building site. As I arrived the lads at work started to clap, and for a few minutes I didn't know why. Then the site manager came up to me and shook my hand.

I realised it could only be because of one thing. 'How did you find out?' I asked.

'When I realised you hadn't come into work, I checked your details and phoned the hostel, because I knew you not being at work was out of character. The guy at the hostel explained what happened. You saved that kid's life.'

'Well, anybody would have done the same,' I mumbled.

'Take the rest of the week off to make sure you're okay,' he said.

I looked at him and replied, 'Thank you for the offer, but I would prefer to work I can't sit in the hostel one minute more than I have to.'

The site manager sighed. 'Well, if you're sure you feel up to it, but don't overdo it.'

'No, I'll take it easy,' I reassured him.

I went straight to social services after work. I really didn't want to stay at the hostel. I didn't want to think too much about what had happened that morning, but I didn't want to stay at the hostel one minute more than I needed to. Nova wasn't available and Frank still wasn't back from his holiday. I could see I was wasting my time. The only person who was going to get me out of that hostel was myself. On the way back to the hostel I was thinking of Maria and my family. If I told them what happened, they'd be worried for my safety, so I decided not to mention anything.

I got back and the police had left a message for me to call them back, which I decided to do straight away. They asked me to give a statement and I agreed. They asked if they could come to the hostel, but I said no because the last thing I needed was any more aggravation with the other residents. I agreed to go to the station after work the next day, where I got the statement done. They told me the woman was being charged with attempted murder, plus various other things that I wasn't interested in. The young lad was doing okay, but the police found drugs on him. They weren't going to charge him for that, but he was on a warning, whatever that means. I asked the police if I would need to be in court, and they said that they hoped not, that if they could get enough evidence she may well plead guilty.

After all that, it was time for me to start thinking about getting out of the hostel. I started looking at rental properties and the costs. The problem for me with renting would be that I wouldn't be able to save much money. I didn't want to do a house share because that wouldn't suit me. Living in the hostel meant I was saving lots of money, which helped with my goal of getting my own house again. The problem was if my family found out that I'd been stabbed because I was trying to help a twelve-year-old who was delivering drugs, Josephine would be so worried, which would mean that Khan and Jon would want me out of the hostel. I understood how they would feel, but I was adamant that I was going to see this out.

I watched TV that night trying to unwind, which was nearly impossible given the day I'd had. I started to think about my nieces, Indiana and Nevada. What if they ever got into the situation that the young lad had gotten himself into? I started to wonder just how he had gotten into that kind of mess. All these things were rolling around my head. I wondered if the young lad was in danger. What if it was his parents that put him up to the job? I should have asked the police more questions. I may have had peace of mind.

I didn't sleep much that night; my nieces were on my mind. I tried to think of nice stuff, like the time I made them the den and they were so happy they cried. I started to think about the den. The den was just what I needed right now, in fact. That would get me out of the hostel, and it wouldn't cost the earth to set up – but where could I put it?

I got up at 3 am and left by 3.30 am. Thankfully there wasn't much action that morning so I managed to get out without any hassle. All that kept going through my mind that day was making myself a den. It would be a hard way of life, but I would be out of that hostel. The more I thought about the idea the more I liked it, so I decided after work I would have a look around for somewhere to set up a den. I would be out of that hostel without costing me too much money, and if I found a suitable area I should be able to stay there as long as I needed.

After work I didn't feel so good – I figured it was the shock, as I wasn't in any pain and my wound wasn't deep, more like a scratch. I couldn't face the hostel that night, and lucky for me I could get out of there, so I decided to go and see Aunt Josephine and stay with her for a night. I wasn't going to tell her or anyone else in my family anything about what had happened the night before, and I hoped they wouldn't find out.

Once Josephine finished work at the shop, we made our way over to the house. It felt really nice to be in a warm, comfortable home, and just walking through the door was the most pleasing experience. I sat on the sofa, and the next thing I knew I was waking up, and Josephine had gone to bed, so I get into my bed.

The next morning I got up, made myself tea and toast and went to work. I didn't see Josephine before I left; she was still asleep. I'm glad I went though, because I felt so much better. I just couldn't face that hostel, especially when I wasn't feeling too good. And after work, I would find somewhere to camp.

I knew camping wasn't ideal and I knew that I didn't have to do this, but I felt it was a good idea, and I would be able to save my money – plus I'd been part of many encampments when I was a soldier. I knew how hard it could be, but that wasn't bothering me. I was more bothered about staying in that hostel.

*

I finished work at noon and went on foot. As I headed out of town I felt like I was on a mission. While I was on my walkabout, I realised that it had been almost twelve months since my release from service. My first twelve months had not been too good in all honesty; in fact it had been a total disaster, but I decided I mustn't dwell on it because it could quite easily push me off the rails, and that would start a downward spiral that I may not ever get out of. I resolved to just look forward and see what is in front of me only.

After ten minutes' walking I reached the edge of town and in front of me lay a wooded area. Looking around, I found a bit of a clearing. There was a lot of litter in this area and I imagined that come the summer, young people would come out there for parties. I walked on for about another twenty minutes, and just on the edge of the wooded area there was an old double-arched footbridge. Running under one of the arches was a stream – it was so clear I could see the rocks laying at the bottom. The sound of this stream, gently flowing to where it going, was so relaxing, so I sat myself down on a large piece of rock, resting my back against a tree, listening to the stream flowing by. I took in my surroundings while I sat there, the spring sun's warmth on my face. The trees were starting to bud and there were daffodils everywhere. I felt like I had found heaven. I must have fallen asleep for a few minutes, and as I woke, I felt a sense of peace. This spot would be perfect for me to set up camp, and I hadn't seen any houses nearby, so I wouldn't be interfering with anybody else.

The bridge must have been put there for a reason, but that reason was unclear to me. When I looked closer, I spotted a plaque that read '1806'. The bridge was beautiful and was going to make an excellent location for me. The fact it had two arches was very handy indeed. The stream passing under one arch would be useful for washing water, and the other arch being dry would help me shelter from the most severe weather. I took one more look around and decided this going to be my place. Then I walked back to my workplace to see how long it would take: just about forty-two minutes – perfect.

My good mood faltered a little when I got back to the hostel and the police were there again. That night it was all kicking off again. After the stabbing, it had been quiet for a few nights, but they must have forgotten about that now, and the addicts were looking for a new drama. I couldn't wait to get out of there. I couldn't stand much more. What got on my nerves the most was they couldn't understand that this place was here just to help them out of their mess. They looked at the place as if it wasn't good enough for them and they somehow deserved better, but they weren't prepared to do anything for themselves except get their drugs and alcohol. Personally, I blamed a lot of these problems on poor parenting. These people had no respect for other people and their properties. They had no respect for the hostel and no respect for the people who run it; it's a completely fucked up system. I have learnt through being there if there is no respect, there is no point, and it's all a waste of time.

After work the next day I went straight to the army and navy surplus store. I explained my situation to the guy, and told him what I needed. He was very understanding and told me.

'That's the best thing you can do,' he said. 'Leave it with me for a couple of days. I'll make a few enquiries and I'm sure I can get you the things you need to make good encampment.'

I felt very pleased with myself for making this decision, and I felt confident in what I was doing.

After a few days, the guy at the surplus store phoned me to tell me he had managed to get his hands on a really good tent and most of the equipment. It wasn't going to be cheap because ex-military equipment is the best quality, but once I bought it I wouldn't have to pay for anything else. Then he texted me the list of equipment he had put together for me.

1. *Four-person tent fully waterproof and top quality groundsheet £545.00*
2. *Best quality military-grade sleeping bag £185.00*
3. *Camp bed and fly net £35.00*
4. *Military standard cooking equipment £89.00*
5. *2 Military standard solar panels £296.00*
6. *4 military standard water containers £84.00*
7. *2 military standard battery lights £48.00*
8. *1 washing facility with shower head £ 210.00*

Optional military-grade radio. £78.00

Total £1,570.00

All this will be ready for collection 22nd March and I ask you for a 20% deposit

After work, I went straight to the shop and paid Dave the 20% deposit. I was worried about telling him that I wouldn't have the full amount straight away.

'Not to worry,' Dave reassured me. 'You can pay when you have the money.'

I felt really grateful.

Dave explained, 'If you can leave it til the weekend I will drop it off for you Saturday morning and help set up.'

'That would be very helpful,' I said, relieved.

Dave knew I didn't want my family to know what I was up to. And he understood my reasons because, as it turned out, Dave himself had been in a similar situation in the past.

*

The week went by pretty quickly, and Saturday soon came around. I didn't tell the hostel or social services what I was doing – all my mail went to Josephine anyway. I intended to leave it a week and see how I got on first. I'd told Maria

I was working Saturday morning – which technically I was, just not at the building site.

I met Dave at the shop on Saturday and, as Dave had promised, his van was already loaded up, and off we went. We couldn't get really close to the spot I'd chosen so we needed a carry the equipment a tidy way, but with the two of us on the job it didn't take too long – and Dave pointed out that it was better if vehicles didn't get too close. We got stuck in and I was set up within a couple of hours. I paid Dave half the money there and then, and told him I hoped to have the other half within the next three months. Dave was happy with that, and it meant I wouldn't be leaving myself short.

Once everything was set up and Dave left, I secured everything as best I could and made my way over to Maria's. I thought it would be useful to leave everything for a couple of days to see if anything got disturbed. The plan for that weekend was the usual routine of being at Maria's, but with Sunday dinner at Khan's place. I loved spending time with Khan, Linda and the girls, as well as Josephine, Alex, Jon, and Fay – we had a lovely day.

After tea, Maria and I left to go back to the cottage. Maria was starting to get excited about her new job and I was very happy for her. I didn't mention any of my problems to her; I didn't want to cause any worry. However, Maria noticed my wound, and she was horrified. I told her it happened at work and it was my own fault. Thankfully she accepted the story and told me to be more careful.

On Monday morning Maria dropped me back at work. I couldn't wait for work to finish so I could get to my den. When I arrived everything was just as I had left it; I was so pleased about that. I stay there that night. Next morning straight to work. After work, I went back to the hostel and picked up my stuff. I didn't tell them I was leaving because I wanted a week at the den first.

On the way back to the den I picked up a few things from the shop. On arrival, I made the den a bit more comfortable, tried out my cooking equipment with some beans on toast – perfect – and felt so much better. I didn't care that I didn't have a TV – the radio was enough for me. When we'd set up the tent, Dave fetched his gardening tools and we cleared the weeds from under the arch so that half my tent was under the bridge, which was giving it good shelter ready for bad weather. The tent felt like a castle to me.

I fetched some water from the stream and set up my washing facility, which, it has to be said, is pretty ingenious. It was only cold water, but I could warm the water with the kettle if needs be, or my other option was to place the container in the sun to warm it, and since the container was fully covered it wouldn't go green.

For the first time since I'd handed over my house keys, I felt organised; my sense of independence was starting to return. This way of life wouldn't be for everyone – remember, I'm a trained soldier who spent fifteen years in the forces, and at various times I was living in tents, so I knew what to expect and how to prepare. Without my military background I wouldn't entertain living like this; you could quite easily die out there if you didn't know what you were doing.

*

The first few weeks went well, and I settled in very easily. I was getting plenty of sleep – no banging, no slamming, no police, no robberies, no drugs under my nose, and the smell of alcohol was gone. It was heaven compared to the hostel after the first week.

141

I went back to the hostel and gave back the keys to my room, explaining I'd moved in with my mother. They didn't ask any questions; they were just glad to have the keys back. I was still doing the early shift at work because I hadn't told my workplace that I'd moved, and one day on my way to work I noticed an advert for a part-time farm hand. I googled the address and it turned out that it wasn't too far from where I was staying, and the bus stopped not too far from the farm.

I decided to give the guy a call because I could get there for 1 pm, and it wasn't like I had anything to do at the tent.

When he answered the phone he seemed to be shouting at me, but I soon realised he couldn't hear me.

'I will call in tomorrow,' I said loudly and clearly.

'That's the best thing,' the guy said, 'because this job is hard work and you need to see if you can work first.'

I felt like telling him that hard work didn't bother me, but I decided to meet him first. If I got two jobs I would be able to save more money.

The next day I finished work, got straight on the bus and went to the farm. When I arrived, I could see the farmhouse was very well kept, just how you would imagine a typical three-storey seventeenth-century old English farmhouse to look. This timber-framed building was very impressive.

I went over to the farmhouse and knocked on the beautiful solid oak door, but nobody answered. I could see some activity going on around the back, so I decided to take a look. When I got round there I could see the farmer was hard at work. He noticed me and stopped, washed his hands and walked over.

'Hello, I'm Edmond,' he said, shaking my hand. He gestured to a woman who had emerged from an outbuilding. 'And this is my wife Sally.'

142

I introduced myself and told them that I was pleased to meet them both. 'I've come about the job. What would you like me to do?'

Edmond looked at me and smiled. 'Get stuck in and do some work – can you do that?'

He looked weary. I couldn't help myself – I started to laugh and said, 'I bet you've had some useless characters here.'

'Worse than useless!' he laughed bitterly. 'We had one young lad – they sent him for work experience. He stood in a pile of cow shit, looked at his trainers, he was mortified and he ran off. We never saw him again, ain't that right, Sal?'

'That's right,' Sally nodded. 'Although some of them do last a full day, and then they'll send their parents to collect their day's pay. And those silly parents will even make excuses for their useless offspring. I'm just glad they're not my children. My children are good workers and very well motivated.'

I liked Edmond and Sally all ready. Edmond was straight-talking and came across as a hard-working man.

I drew a deep breath and decided it was my turn to be straight-talking. 'Edmond, Sally, before we go any further, I best let you know I'm a plumber by trade and I have a job on a building site. I start at 4 am and finish at 12 noon, so I can be here by 1 pm each day. I prefer not to work weekends, but if you're stuck give me two week's notice and I will do the weekend for you and book a Monday off work.'

Sally looked concerned. 'Will you be able to manage the two jobs?'

'I don't have any choice. I'm in financial difficulties, and I'm doing my best to get out of the mess.'

'When can you start?' Edmond asked.

'Now,' I replied, 'if you've got something for me to do.'

Edmond smiled and said, 'We've always got something to do.'

'Okay, where would you like me to start?'

I started work on the farm that day, and I've never looked back since. As promised, I got there every day at 1 pm, and Sally always had a sandwich and a cup of tea waiting for me. After the first few months I started to enjoy being on the farm more than being a plumber. I soon learnt how to drive the machinery, feed the cattle, clean the sheds, plough the fields, harvest the crops. Edmond was an excellent teacher and for the first time in my life I felt like I had a father figure. Edmond had plenty of patience and taught me well. I was the most content I'd ever been. The long summer nights were excellent for farming work, and some days I would be there until 8 pm.

A few times Edmond said, 'Don't you have a home to go to?'

I'd laugh along with him while thinking to myself, 'Not yet, but someday soon.' I didn't tell them the truth about where I was living. It seemed strange because I felt very happy despite my homelessness. I was happy because I had Maria, happy because I'd moved out of the hostel, and yes I was living rough but it didn't feel like that after the hostel. I told myself it was part of a training exercise for a better life. Maria had started her new job with the magazine, and she was very happy because it was more up to date than the paper, plus now she spent more time looking for good news and positive stuff. My family still didn't know that I had moved out of the hostel, and that's just how I wanted it to stay. I was getting on very well with Edmond and Sally, and my money was coming together nicely – I was making great progress with my savings. I felt like my life was starting to go places again.

Edmond and Sally had a daughter called Jane and a son called Walter. They visited their parents regularly and always made a point of coming to chat to me. They were both genuinely nice people. Jane worked in London with HSBC, and reading between the lines she was quite high up in the ranks and very well paid. Walter was a teacher in a school in Gloucestershire, married with three children. I got the impression that neither Jane nor Walter were interested in the farm. They did come and help when they were most needed, but that was only out of concern for Edmond and Sally. Walter told me that he wanted his parents to retire but that they wouldn't hear of it. Edmond told me himself, 'A farmer never retires, he just drives the tractor to the end of the field.' I could see that the farm was too much for Edmond and Sally; I'd realised that the first day I'd arrived. But none of this was any of my business, and I tried not to get involved. I was just happy to have the job and, best of all, a job I liked doing.

As we got close to harvest both Jane and Walter stayed at the farm for a while, and I was glad they did because the work was hard and the days were long. The nights were starting to get colder, and I started to light my fire most nights. I always tried to do it after dark so that nobody would notice the smoke.

Maria and I were still getting on very well, and I longed for us to be back together in our own place again. If my work continued at this rate, come May we could start looking for our own place again, because having the two jobs had given me a much-needed boost. I kept my focus on the goal and that kept me going. Living in the tent through December and January took its toll on me, and it must have started to show, because one day Edmond told me I didn't look well. In fact, he actually asked me if I was living rough, to which I quickly replied no. But I knew Edmond was no fool. This worried me slightly because I could see he was genuinely concerned, and the last thing I needed was to blow my cover because it would only be another four and half months, five at the most, and I knew I could do it. What was hard was working weekends at the farm, because I would get those couple of days in the warm with a proper bed.

I could see Edmond was making mental notes regarding me. He came up to me one day and asked if I was in trouble. I assured him that as long as I keep working everything would be fine. Edmond had also asked me about my background – not being nosy, just out of interest.

I really liked both Edmond and Sally. They were good family people and good to me, and I truly enjoyed being with and working for them. When I worked weekends Sally always insisted I have dinner with them, which I have to confess I thoroughly enjoyed. Working at the farm had also made living in the tent easy because I was only there to sleep, and by the time Sally had fed me with her sandwiches the size of doorstops I didn't need to cook that much.

Don't get me wrong – living in the tent was no walk in the park, but it was a means to an end. I couldn't have stayed at the hostel for much longer. It was clean, but after the stabbing, that place wasn't for me. The worst thing of all about that situation was the child delivering drugs – that's not what I wanted to see, and neither did anybody else. This can be a wicked world sometimes. After living in the hostel I honestly couldn't see any difference between drugs and alcohol. I do think drugs should be legalised, as this would stop endless crime. But I suppose there is a good reason as to why they're not legal, and that's something I can never change.

*

One cold February Saturday morning I woke early as I'd promised to help out at the farm. I woke up to icy cold air all around me, and I quickly jumped up and put on my warm clothes. As I came out of the tent I noticed that everything was white, and the air was fresh. I took a deep breath and filled my lungs with this cold, fresh air. I put my little gas kettle, which was frozen, on to boil. After a few minutes, I poured myself a cup of tea and sat down on my little chair, wrapping my cold hands around the warm cup, and despite the cold I felt as free as a bird. It's hard living, but at the same time, it's the good life.

When I arrived Edmond was waiting for me, which was unlike him. Normally when I arrived Edmond was working already. He said to me in a slightly stern tone of voice, 'Have you walked here this morning?'

Not thinking, I replied 'Yes.'

Edmond looked me straight in the eye and nodded his head.'

I felt uncomfortable. 'Is everything okay?'

Edmond looked at me with a solemn look and said, 'I hope so.'

I didn't reply, and he said nothing more, so I got to work. I didn't think too much about it after that – I just got stuck in with my work.

After dinner, Edmond told me he was going out and asked if I'd be okay to finish up the day's work on my own. That wasn't a problem for me. Just before he left, though, he stopped, and turned his head in my direction. 'How long did it take you to walk here this morning?'

Not thinking, I said, 'Twenty minutes.'

Edmond nodded his head and said, 'Very good.'

After I'd finished my work I went to see Sally. We always had a cup of tea before I left for the day. I kept expecting Edmond to walk in through the door as he usually appeared before too long, but he was nowhere to be seen.

As I left the farm it was just getting dark, and I noticed Edmond's pickup truck parked by the cow shed.

As I trudged back to the tent I considered the conversations of the day, and how I could stop Edmond from being so worried about me – but I soon stopped when I saw that my fire was already burning and my tent lights were on. I started to panic, and I kept moving forward slowly so I could get a better look at who'd commandeered my tent. I squinted to see who was sitting at the campfire.

It was Edmond.

Then everything came together – the questions, Edmund's pickup parked by the cow shed.

I walked up to the fire, preparing to hear his angry words.

'Sit down. I've just put the kettle on,' he said.

Stunned, I did as he suggested.

'Your family don't know you're living out here, do they?' he asked.

'No,' I confirmed, 'and that's the way I would like it to stay.'

'Your secret's safe with me.'

I nodded in appreciation.

'You know,' Edmond said eventually, 'I was much like you as a young man. I admire your endurance, your ability to work. You're a very focused, determined young man. But I'm not going to lie to you – I'm not happy about this

148

living arrangement. I can see you're very well organised and your setup here is very good. But there isn't any need for this.'

I started to feel slightly annoyed with Edmond. He'd given the impression he'd understood, but maybe not. I quickly replied, 'Look, the truth is I've got fifteen years' service, managed to save enough money to buy my own place, meet the love of my life, and everything was going so well. Then I answered my phone one day to scammers and they took everything from me. I felt such a fool, completely defeated. The strong man that I had become through my fifteen years' service had all come to nothing. Can you imagine how I felt?' I gestured around me, at the tent, the camp. 'This is my way of getting myself back together and coming out of it even stronger than I went in.'

Edmond looked at me and said, 'I fully understand.'

I told Edmond, 'I have a really good family who have offered their support at every stage of my downfall, but I'm determined to put myself back on the map without help or charity. I'm a very proud man. My mother was a very good teacher and made me who I am.'

'What about your father?'

I wouldn't have mentioned him, but now you have, I will tell you. My mother, Josephine, adopted me because my father ran off with a woman half his age, and I was born out of that affair. My natural mum ran off when I was about two years old, leaving me behind. A birthday card once a year is all I've ever had from her. After my father left Josephine for Fannie – my natural mum – Josephine already had four children with my father. Josephine wouldn't ever forgive him, and I don't blame her. So after Fannie left my father, Josephine wouldn't have my father back. He then went on a downward spiral and never recovered. He was devastated when my natural mum left him, not because he was in love with her, but because of what he'd given up to be with her.'

Edmond nodded, listening intently.

'Josephine didn't really want me at first,' I continued. 'This I know because once I was old enough Khan told me the full story. Josephine and my family have been totally honest with me. It was my brothers and sisters that wanted me because they didn't want me to grow up with strangers, so for their benefit Aunt Josephine took me in. Josephine has been the best mother anybody could ever wish for, and I love her with all my heart. She made my life fantastic without any resentment. She told me that adopting me was the best thing she'd ever done, apart from having her own children, and I couldn't wish for anything more, that I'm sure of. They picked me up from the children's home and I was homeless – literally. Khan called me a homeless bear. And here I am again, a homeless bear. Once I get back on my feet this time I will do my utmost to ensure I'm never a homeless bear again. I will work as hard as I can.'

'Good man,' Edmond said encouragingly. He could tell that this was a tough story for me to tell.

'With regards to my father, he's never recovered. He ruined his life for a gold-digger half his age. And he is the kind of person I never want to be. He stays away from all five children because he is overwhelmed with guilt.'

Edmond asked, 'Do you see your natural mother?'

'No, and I would prefer not to. I believe she is married for the third time to some old fool with plenty of money. The only thing I know is that after me, she never had any more children.'

Edmond said, 'I can see you're a very strong man, and I truly admire you working all the hours possible. You're doing well, keeping two jobs going.'

'Listen, you won't tell Sally about where I'm living, will you?'

Edmond shifted on his camping chair. 'I'm here because Sally was concerned for you,' he said. 'She's been telling me for weeks that you're living rough, and it was her idea that I came and looked for myself. She also worked out where you would be camped out, because believe it or not Sally's parents had a house nearby, and Sally and her sisters would play on this bridge. She used to bring the kids here too, when they were little, so she knows all too well how long it takes to walk to the farm from here.'

I'd screwed my face up as I cringed at how naïve I'd been to believe they wouldn't realise something was up.

'Hey, listen,' Edmond said, patting my arm with the back of his hand. 'Don't worry, because Sally has had a tough life, and she understands hardship. She won't look at you any different.'

'In all honesty, I'm glad you've come found me. I don't like being dishonest,' I said.

Edmond smiled. 'I would have done exactly the same thing. You should be very proud of yourself. And Josephine and your family have done an excellent job. Josephine sounds like a very brave woman.'

'Oh, she is.'

Edmond stretched, and slowly stood up. 'Right, I'm going to make my way now, before it gets too dark.'

I thanked Edmond for coming to see me and reminded him that I didn't want my family to know where I was.

'Your secret's safe with me,' he said as he left.

I felt grateful for his company, and I felt much happier

now he knew the truth. Our conversation was very pleasant and I was very grateful that Edmond didn't patronise me – he just admired me, and that made me feel for the first time that I was doing the right thing. Sally was such a nice person and I felt even more grateful to her. I was looking forward to getting back to the farm now that they both knew the truth.

Chapter Nine

❦

In the past few months, I hadn't spent much time with my sisters and I felt guilty about that, so I made arrangements to take them both for dinner – nothing expensive, just an excuse to meet up, really. The following Monday my plumbing job was moving to a new housing development and I couldn't start at my usual 4 am. My boss said after the first week he would try and get it sorted for me.

It was a bit of a blow, to be honest, because I couldn't get to the farm and do my hours there. Edmond was understanding on the phone and told me not to worry, but I did. I knew full well that Edmond and Sally couldn't manage on their own. So what I did was work through lunch, and I managed to get finished at 4 pm and went straight over to the farm. I just had this feeling that I needed to be there for some reason.

As I arrived I saw an ambulance parked outside the farmhouse and my heart missed a beat. I ran straight in there, Sally told me how they thought Edmond suffered a heart attack.

I told Sally I was really sorry.

'It's not your fault,' she said. 'I told Edmond not to overdo it today, but you know what he's like. He's a stubborn old fool, he is.'

I rang my site manager straight away and told him that

I wasn't going to be able to work for the next few days. Then I told Sally not to worry about the farm as I would take care of everything. I could see the relief on her face as she thanked me.

Jane and Walter soon arrived, and they were understandably both very worried.

Once Sally had the support of her children I slipped into the background and got on with the day-to-day running of the farm. I really wished I had told my site manager I could only do my regular hours as that way I would have been able to work at the farm that day. It's not to say this wouldn't have happened if I'd been there, but I would have felt much better with myself knowing I was there.

*

After running all the tests and checks, the hospital confirmed that Edmond had suffered a minor heart attack, and the next couple of months were crucial, and he'd need to take things easy because it could happen again, and next time it could be worse. The good news was that all his arteries were clear, and no further treatment was needed, so he could return home.

Walter decided to stay at the farm for a couple of weeks, which I was relieved about. Walter's wife Maggie also stayed over with the children, but only at the weekend because of school – Maggie was a teacher and couldn't have much time off work. Sally, ever the true farmer's wife, spent more time out of the house and helping with all the physical work on the farm as well as seeing to Edmond's every need.

My site manager quickly made arrangements for me to be able to start at 4 am, which I was grateful for.

After two weeks' rest, Edmond started to show his face outside again, but only for a couple of hours each day,

154

doctor's orders. I could clearly see what had happened had really shaken him up.

Spring was starting to creep up on us by then, and my life in the tent was starting to get easier again – although I longed for May to arrive as I needed the milder air on my face. The cold air takes its toll and I could see that Josephine was starting to notice that my appearance was increasingly rough. I explained that it was because of the many hours of outdoor work, and to be honest maybe there was some truth in that.

Aunt Josephine accepted my story and told me that she would be glad when I was back on my feet. Maria was on more money than in her previous job. Between the two of us, we'd managed to save just over £25,000. I felt very pleased to know that we were getting somewhere, but we would need to keep up the pace for a while longer yet. I worked it out that if I could manage another twelve months in the tent, we'd be well ahead of ourselves.

Of course, Maria didn't know I was living in a tent, but she really wanted us to be together, the sooner the better. I missed her like mad, but I just kept thinking how the more money we could save, the smaller the mortgage repayments would be.

As the days were getting warmer I noticed Edmond was getting back to his old self, which in turn took the pressure off me, and meant I could start enjoying the farming life again. Walter had been helping out most weekends, but he told me himself that he couldn't spare many more weekends because he was starting to fall behind with work and finances.

One early Saturday morning in mid May, I arrived at the farm as usual, and Edmond called me into the farmhouse. This was unlike him – normally I just started work, and then we'd have coffee and a quick chat at around 10.30 am. As I walked in, Sally asked me to sit down, and this, for me, was an indication that something serious was heading my way. I felt uncertain and felt myself getting hot. My head quickly started to fill with all kinds of thoughts, which started to race around at a million miles an hour, and the one thought that stood out the most was that I hoped Edmond and Sally hadn't sold the farm. I knew Walter and Jane weren't interested, and I knew Edmond had been unwell. I felt extremely disappointed, like I was just about to take another blow. I felt like the chair somehow was holding me in position, ready to take the blow. I kept thinking to myself, 'Please don't tell me you're selling the farm.'

Sally filled the kettle, and Edmond started to talk. 'Me and Sally have been thinking – and that don't happen very often,' he said with a smile. 'We both can see how happy you are on the farm. We've had years of experience with farmhands, and every hard-working farmhand like you has gone on to be very successful with their own farms.'

I couldn't see where this was going, so I stayed silent, eyes on Edmond, waiting for whatever was coming.

'So, before you leave us, we want to put an offer on the table here for you. And before I go any further, let me tell you Walter and Jane have agreed to this.'

I was very unsure I what was coming next and I felt very anxious.

Sally put three cups of tea on the table and sat down.

Edmond continued, 'I would like you to listen to what I have to say before you say anything.'

The suspense was excruciating. I nodded, eager to know what was coming.

'We are both aware that you need a home, and we are

getting too old to manage this farm the way we'd like it to be managed. Within the boundaries of our farm, we have planning permission to build a house, which we applied for just over three years ago because Walter was going to build the house for himself. However, overnight Walter's plans changed because he got a better job than he was expecting. Walter then decided to leave because it was in all honesty an excellent opportunity. We still have just under two years to start building the house before planning permission runs out. If you could see your way clear to building a house – and yes I'm aware it's a tall order, but with your determination, I'm sure you could do just about anything – you should be able to get a mortgage to buy the farm without the farmhouse. I say without the farmhouse because we still want to live here on the farm, and myself and Sally could help you out if you need us, and that way we can keep active doing something we love doing. And the farm is worth a lot less without the original house, which would help you out. We would need to retain one acre of the land that sits around the house because that would be for Walter and Jane to inherit, and that one acre would make the house worth a lot more money. You wouldn't need the one acre because you would have built yourself a new farmhouse.'

Edmond appeared to have gotten to the end of his proposal, and I was figuring out what to say when he put both hands up. 'I don't want you to say anything now. I want you to think about what I've said, and we will chat again after the weekend.'

I couldn't believe what I was hearing. I felt so excited inside and I wanted to jump up and shout YES! But Edmond was right – there was a lot to think about, and talk can be cheap.

I thanked them both for their consideration, and for having faith in me, and we started work – but it was hard for me to concentrate. I was glad when the working day was done, which was unlike me.

I got back to my tent. I knew it was a cold night because I felt the ground crunching under my feet, but that night I couldn't feel the cold – I couldn't feel anything.

I couldn't wait to tell Maria. I felt like our struggle may well be coming to an end finally. But before I phoned anybody, I started to think about how I could make this work. I needed a plan in place before I spoke to anyone.

*

That night everything was going through my head, and it was so cold, so I just couldn't sleep. I decided to go for a walk to shake off the jitters. I sat myself down by a tree and watched the sun rise, serenaded by the whistling birds, deep in thought. The March sun warmed my face and I fell asleep.

When I woke up, I had a plan. I needed to speak to Khan and Jon. I quickly made my way back to the tent, picked up a few things and made my way over to Josephine's. On my way over, I phoned Khan and Jon and asked if they had time to meet at some point that weekend and we made plans to meet at Josephine's after 6 that evening, which was perfect because I was taking Maria for lunch. I got to Josephine's, put the washing machine on and had a shower. Josephine was at the shop, giving me a chance to get cleaned up before I saw her. Maria was picking me up at one and we had a table booked for two, though she arrived early and we had a couple of hours chilling out, spending precious time together. I decided not to tell Maria that Edmond and Sally had offered me a good opportunity until I had spoken to Khan and Jon. I didn't want to build her hopes up.

We had a lovely afternoon – the hotel we dined in was luxurious and comfortable. After lunch, the sun was still warm and the grounds of the hotel were stunning, so we found a place to sit in the sun on the terrace. I could have sat there forever.

I'd told Maria I was meeting Khan and Jon that night about a new job, which in a way I was. Maria dropped me back at Josephine's place, and I told her that I wouldn't get back to the cottage until late. I sat for a while on my own before Khan and Jon arrived, thinking I really wanted to get out of my situation right away. I missed Maria terribly, and being with her that afternoon made me realise that I just could not live for much longer without her by my side.

Khan arrived first, then Jon five minutes later. I made them both a cup of tea, and then I told them what Edmond and Sally had offered me, and the reasons behind it. Both Khan and Jon were delighted for me, and they agreed that it was a very good offer and opportunity.

'So, how can we help you?' Khan asked.

'Yes, how can we help you?' echoed Jon, 'because we can't let this opportunity pass you by.'

I felt so grateful. 'I knew you'd say that. I wondered if you'd be able to support me in building the house.'

Without hesitation, Khan said, 'Yes, how much will you need?'

'I don't think I need any money. I've managed to save around twenty-five thousand after tax.'

'Wow! Well done to you!' Jon exclaimed. How have you managed that much?'

'I've had two jobs for several months. I start work at 4 am and finish most days between 6 pm and 8 pm. I've been saving over a thousand pounds every week.'

Jon's jaw was nearly on the floor, but then he smiled. 'Well done to you.'

Khan sat thinking and then after a few minutes he said, 'If we – us three – work together at weekends and any spare time, we could build a house between the three of us.

'That's a good idea,' Jon said.

'What do you think, Sean?' Khan asked.

'I was hoping you were going to say exactly that,' I confessed. 'I reckon I should have enough money to build the house and get it watertight. Then we could do the inside whenever we can afford to.'

Khan said, 'This is a brilliant opportunity and a brilliant idea. And by Edmond taking the farmhouse out of the deal it makes the farm more affordable for you, and he doesn't lose anything, because so long as the farmhouse has land around it, the house will always be worth the money. It's such a good idea.'

Jon asked, 'Do you get on well with Edmond and Sally?'

'Oh, yes. I get on really well with them. They have been good to me and I tow line as well the work on the farm. It's hard, but I really enjoy it. To be honest, I thought that I liked being a plumber, but then when I started on the farm, I liked that so much more, and now I really want to be a farmer.'

My brothers stood listening, nodding. I was so excited to not have to keep any secrets any more, so I continued.

'Edmond is a very good teacher. I've learnt so much in such a short space of time. Once I'd got back on my feet I was going to ask for a full-time job on the farm anyway. So when Edmond came up with this idea I could have kissed him.'

Khan laughed. 'Okay, well, now we have a plan. We will

build the house between the three of us, which will be the new farmhouse. Once the house is built, you've then got to get a mortgage to buy the farm.'

'Perfect,' I beamed.

'Jon what are you thinking?' asked Khan.

'We, all three of us, need to go and meet Edmond and Sally, to confirm that's definitely what they want to do. I'll then draw up the plans for the new farmhouse, and before we start the build I think the best option would be to visit the banks and make sure there will be a mortgage available, and at what cost.' Jon looked at me. 'I don't doubt that you'll get a mortgage, but we need to get everything covered, because the last thing we want is for you to endure any more setbacks.'

'That's right,' said Khan. 'I don't wish to upset you, Sean, but in the last six months this situation has really taken its toll on you.'

'Yes,' Jon said sternly. 'I've noticed you've started to look somewhat withdrawn, so truth be told we don't want to put you any further down.' Then Jon's face softened. 'I'm really glad you've come to us though.'

Khan said, 'Okay, Sean, first things first, let's get organised. When you go back to the farm on Monday, arrange a meeting with Edmond, Sally and us three, so that myself and Jon can help with the planning. I would also speak to Walter and Jane yourself. That way when we start the ball rolling we can be running on all cylinders.'

We decided on suggesting a meeting at 6 pm on Wednesday.

I told Khan and Jon, 'Listen though – I don't want Mother or Maria to know until we have a deal in place.'

Khan said, 'That's a good idea. Let's not tell any of the women so that we don't cause any trouble.' Then he paused for a moment, seeming to weigh up whether to say whatever was on his mind. 'Sean, I have to know. What made you change your mind about us helping you? Because at first, you wouldn't accept any offer of help. What's changed your mind?'

I looked at Khan and said, 'I'm sick of working very hard and living rough, and you're both right – it's taking its toll on my health.' I never gave any indication of just how rough I'd been living. 'And this is a once-in-a-lifetime opportunity. I know I couldn't do this without your support. As independent as I like to be, I know full well I cannot sort all this out on my own without it costing me more money than I can afford, and I've lost so much already.'

Khan and Jon nodded, relieved that I'd finally come to my senses. 'More importantly,' I continued, 'Maria and I would like to be together again permanently. These last few months have been so torturous for us both, so it would be selfish of me to miss this opportunity by trying to be so independent.'

Khan said, 'It's very sensible. You've done the right thing, and we'll do everything we can to help you.'

'That's right,' said Jon. 'And now that you've managed to save a decent amount, it's only mine and Khan's time you need, so you *are* still independent. We're proud of you, mate. I don't for one minute imagine any of this has been easy, and you've coped very well. Mother was worried that this episode of your life was going to break you – because of Father's history.'

I felt so grateful to Khan and Jon. Not only did they support my idea but they were prepared to help me too. I felt so blessed. Their support gave me the confidence I needed to move forward.

On Monday I got to the farm at 1 pm as usual, and as ever, Sally was waiting with a cup of tea and a sandwich for me. Edmond was outside, so once I'd eaten I got straight to work. I got in the tractor and started to clean the barns and the cow shed. For the first time in a long time, I felt a sense of contentment. There wasn't anything I wanted to do more than be on this farm.

I started thinking back to my situation and what had happened to me, and how I had found myself now. I thought I was happy and had everything I wanted back at our place – but If I hadn't have lost our place, I might never have found life on the farm. People sometimes say every cloud has a silver lining, and I for one believe that to be true – but only if you're looking. If you stand still, you'll never find anything. Lesson to myself: nothing comes easy.

After all the work was done, Edmond invited me over to the house, where Sally joined us at the kitchen table.

'Have you had time to think about our offer?' Sally asked the moment we were all sat down.

'Yes,' I began. 'I met with my brothers on Sunday afternoon, because obviously this is a big move for me. I can't afford any more mistakes, so I need their advice. Both Khan and Jon are doing very well. Khan is an electrician and Jon is a specialist builder, and both run their own businesses.'

'They sound very interesting, and very knowledgeable,' Edmond said.

'They are, and I need their knowledge and help if I'm going to take the farm on. And they're both prepared to help me. In fact, they've asked me to arrange a meeting for Wednesday at 6 pm with both of you if that's okay?'

Edmond glanced at Sally and they both nodded. 'Yes, of course,' he replied.

'Great. Do you think Walter and Jane could also come along then?'

Sally replied, 'Jane will, but not Walter. He'll be working then.'

'Sean, can I ask: are you definitely interested?' Edmond said.

'Yes. I'm really interested. This is an incredible opportunity for me. Jon will be able to sort out the architect's drawings and plans, which will be a massive help. Both of my brothers will help me with the construction on weekends and in any spare time. However, they want to go through everything with you and Sally so that we are all happy, before Jon starts with the plans.'

'And that's happening Wednesday?' Edmond said.

'Yes, if that's okay with you both, and Jane.'

They both nodded, and Sally smiled, her eyes teary.

*

Wednesday soon arrived and it was time for us all to meet. Jon already had a draft plan to put forward – he'd been on Google Maps to look at the farm's layout. He'd also spoken to a mortgage company that he worked with.

I was surprised to see Walter when we entered the farmhouse. He'd been able to get out of work early and he looked excited to see me.

The meeting started with friendly chatter about this and that, and everyone got familiar with each other, and then we got onto the business at hand.

Edmond started things off. 'I want to sell the farm but retain the farmhouse with one acre of land. Also, I reckon the entrance to the farm will need to be changed so that we're not in each other's way.'

I nodded. So far so good.

'So, excluding the existing farmhouse, I have forty-two acres, five barns, two tractors, and everything else you need to make the farm work, including the cattle. That's all been valued at £450,000 total.'

Jon raised his eyebrows and looked at Edmond. 'That's more than I expected.'

'What were you expecting?' Edmond enquired.

Jon said, 'To be honest, I thought we'd be looking at something like £380,000, which for Sean would be plain sailing. Don't take this the wrong way, but are you willing to take a hit on your asking price?'

Edmond took a sharp breath in. 'I wasn't expecting to "take a hit", as you put it.'

His tone of voice was slightly abrupt. I felt uncomfortable.

Jon, however, wasn't fazed. 'What's the annual turnover?'

'Well ... right now it's between eighty and ninety thousand a year, but I'm sure Sean would be able to achieve much more. Young blood is what's needed on this farm. In recent years I've fallen behind, so I believe my asking price is fair.'

'I'm sure you understand that I need to ask such questions,' Jon said.

Still uneasy, I looked across at Khan, but he was having a separate conversation with Jane and Walter and didn't notice my glance.

Jon told me, 'I'm going to have to draw you a fantastic farmhouse in order to get the mortgage you need. But I believe after speaking to my mortgage guy today, once all the plans are submitted – which I'm going to do through my company – we should be able to get the mortgage on the strength of the plans, because I've worked with the same company for years and we have a very good working relationship. Without sounding too clever, I should be able to get the money sooner rather than later.'

Khan spoke up at that point. 'So the farm and all equipment that you currently use to run the farm is four hundred and fifty thousand, without one acre of land and the farmhouse?'

Edmond nodded. 'Yes.'

I felt very grateful to my brothers. I can do the physical work, but the business and finance side of things I found much more difficult.

I thought to myself how once this meeting was over, and if everything went to plan, I would need to bring Maria on board. Maria knew how I felt about my job on the farm, so she would understand why I would be interested in owning my own farm.

Jon was writing everything down, and he'd printed a map, and Edmond was showing him the boundaries of the farm.

'What about neighbours? Are there any problems with neighbouring farms?' Jon asked.

Edmond said, 'No. I get along with everyone.'

This question had never entered my head. I was so lucky that Jon was my brother.

'Who would be your solicitor, and are they aware of the proposal?' Jon asked next.

Edmond pulled out a business card, handed it to Jon and said, 'Yes, we've notified them.'

'I'll also need your audited accounts,' Jon continued. He was in his element.

Edmond pulled out another card at this point, and Jon gave Edmond a card in return and asked if his accountant could email across the accounts for the last two years.'

Edmond said, 'Of course. I'll ask them.'

Everything was going very smoothly, but for some reason I felt like that wasn't going to last. The truth was that everything that had happened to me over the past several months had taken its toll.

After Jon's notebook was almost full, the meeting was coming to an end. Edmond and Sally had a look of relief on their faces. Khan and Jon were ready to leave and they offered to drop me back at the hostel. I told them I was staying at the farm that night to help with the lambing. They accepted my excuse without any questions, and for that I was grateful.

After they left, Sally told me the spare room was ready.

I really didn't want to go back to the tent that night, so I accepted her kind offer.

*

The next day I was up and gone before anybody else was awake. I phoned Maria and asked her if she could pick me up from the farm after 5 pm, and she agreed. I wanted her to have a good look around and for me to explain what I was hoping to do. Maria was already aware that I was enjoying my time on the farm. She had met Edmond and Sally before, but only once.

I finished at the building site, went over to the farm and started my second job. Maria arrived as planned, at just after 5 pm, and pulled up, engine running. I walked over and asked her if she would take a look around.

'I thought I was just picking you up?' she said, frowning.

'Yes, you are picking me up, but there's something I want to show you,' I replied.

We walked around the back of the cow shed, and up the

gentle slope behind it, which gave a really good view of the land. By that point, Maria had a worried look on her face, so I decided it was time to start talking.

'Nothing's wrong. I just want to show you something. You see, all this land?'

Maria looked around impatiently. 'Yes, of course I can see this land.'

I carried on. 'If everything goes to plan, this will all be ours.'

Maria scoffed. 'Stop being silly. Come on, let's go.' She turned to walk back down towards the car.

'I'm not being silly. Khan and Jon were here last night, helping me to sort out the details. Look, Maria – you see that piece of land just over there, with the wire fence? Well, that's where I'm going to build a new farmhouse.'

Maria looked at me, looked at the land, looked back at me, and started to cry. 'Please don't put us in dreamland. I know you mean well, but honestly, it's not helping.'

I groaned in frustration. 'I knew you wouldn't believe me. That's why I asked you to pick me up. Come on, let's go and see Sally and Edmond, and they can explain.'

As we walked into the farmhouse, Sally greeted us and asked if we wanted a cup of tea, and we sat down. I could see Maria was a bit bewildered and very uncomfortable, and I started to think I shouldn't have told her like this.

Just then, Edmond walked in. He looked at Maria, then me, and said, 'Is everything okay?'

I replied 'Yes, but Maria's struggling to believe what I have just told her.'

Edmond wasn't anybody's fool; he knew exactly what I was talking about. He looked at Maria and said, 'We – myself and Sally – have become very attached to Sean, and

168

we are amazed at the determination he has to get back on his feet.'

Maria was still looking very anxious.

Edmond carried on. 'I don't know if he's mentioned this to you, but I've not been feeling well, and that means I've got to slow down. The farm is very hard work. In truth, it's a young man's game, and as you can see I'm not as young as I'd like to think I am. We're selling this place and, hopefully, if everything goes well, Sean is our buyer.'

Maria looked in shock and for a moment, clearly lost for words. Then she looked at Sally. 'But where will you live?'

Sally laughed and gestured to the room around her. 'In here. We're not selling the farmhouse, just the farm and all the equipment.'

Maria still looking very puzzled turned to me and said, 'Sean, I think we'd better get back to my place now.'

Edmond said, 'You don't believe us, do you?'

Maria quickly replied, 'I believe that you're selling this farm, but I don't believe we have the money to buy it.'

Edmond smiled. 'Maybe not, but between myself, Sally, Sean and Sean's brothers, we're hoping to get it sorted out.'

'Perhaps we could see Jon and he could explain,' I suggested.

'Good idea,' Sally said. She looked at Maria and added, 'Don't look so worried. There isn't anything to worry about.'

Maria replied, 'Sean loves working here, and I don't want him to lose his job.' Maria paused for a moment, looking into the distance. 'My mother always told me illusions of grandeur are bad for the health.'

Edmond chuckled warmly. 'I totally agree with your mother.'

169

As we said our goodnights and left, I could see Edmond and Sally were finding this all very amusing.

As we drove away from the farm I asked Maria if she wanted to visit Khan or Jon so they could explain, but Maria wasn't in the mood right then. I could see that she was going to take some convincing.

'Have you won the lottery?' she asked, suspiciously.

'I wish. But I have managed to save just over twenty-five thousand pounds.'

'How much?!'

'I've had two jobs, Maria, and I haven't stopped working. I need a lot more than twenty-five thousand pounds for the farm, but Edmond has come up with a generous plan which will help me to buy the farm. Also, Jon and Khan are going to help me.'

'Help you? In what way?'

'In the deal, Edmond and Sally retain the farmhouse plus one acre of land that sits around it. This will then take a lot of the value out of the farm. Myself, Khan and Jon will build a new farmhouse in line with the one Edmond has got planning permission for.'

Maria took a long breath. 'This is too much to take in for one day, Sean.'

'I get that. But can you do one thing for me? Try not to worry and trust me when I say I'll, sort everything out for us. I promised you when we left our first home that I will get back on my feet – and I meant it.'

Maria was silent, but when I glanced at her she was in floods of tears.

'Why are you crying? You're not happy?'

'I'm more than happy, Sean. I'm amazed at how well you've done. I thought this situation would go on for years.'

170

I was relieved to hear this. 'Let's just keep it to ourselves for the time being, just in case anything goes wrong.'

Maria nodded. 'Of course. I thought you were joking when you first told me, and I felt so embarrassed. Even when Edmond told me I thought he was trying to make you look good. I'm really sorry for doubting you, but it seems such a big step.'

'It is a big step, you're right. Without the support of my brothers, and Edmond and Sally, I would never be able to take on the farm.'

'Do you know something?' she said. 'I love the farm. When I was a little girl, I spent loads of time over at our farms.'

'Really? You never mentioned it before.'

'Yeah, I thought it might put you under pressure if I brought it up. I was really happy for you when you started working on the farm because I knew how happy I was helping out on our farm. The couple who rented my father's cattle farm had children my age, and some weekends and summer holidays I would stay over. As I got older I would help them out, so I learnt a lot from them. Once you started to tell me about your job on the farm, it reminded me about my childhood and happy times on the farm.'

I could see it in my head – a young Maria mucking in with all the jobs.

She continued, 'I did out of curiosity check the tenancy agreements with my father's farms, but they had both been renewed pretty recently. However, at one time, my father had trouble, after Peter and Lou left, getting someone else in to manage the farm – and my father doesn't take much rent either. But anyway, I honestly cannot believe that this is really happening. I feel so proud of you.'

'Well, we have a long way to go,' I said, 'so let's try not to get too excited. I feel very lucky though, to even have the opportunity. But I can tell you for sure that I wouldn't be able to do this without the backing of my brothers. When I asked Khan and Jon to help, I didn't realise just how much help I was going to need, which is probably a good thing because if I'd known, I wouldn't have put this on my brothers. I could see Jon was on a mission last night, so I dare say he will have something up his sleeve. But anyway Maria, said let's just stay positive and keep our fingers crossed.'

Chapter Ten

❧

In the next few weeks, Jon visited the farm many times with his surveyor. Jon wasn't completely happy with the plans for the new farmhouse, so he changed the design slightly and resubmitted the plans. Jon told me that the new farmhouse needed to be more like the old farmhouse. When I saw the new plans I understood what he meant. I suppose for Walter it would have been fine because the farm would never have been split, so the value was always going to be there. But Jon knew just what he was doing; the new farmhouse looked more like a farmhouse instead of a basic dwelling. The downside, Jon told me, was that resubmitting plans meant any building work would be delayed by at least six months – and that meant another winter in the tent. That was going to be a struggle. I told myself I had to keep going, and that everything was moving in the right direction, although it seemed too slow for me.

Within a week the whole family was aware of my newly acquired status, as was Maria's family. Josephine phoned me to ask about all the details and let me know that if I needed any money she was willing to help, which was good to know.

After a month or so Jon called me into his office as he wanted to go over everything with me. He also had some good news regarding the planning: the council had come back to him with a few questions, and they were confident that they couldn't foresee any problems. Jon also informed me that to secure the mortgage I needed life insurance, and I needed to write my will. To get that part sorted, Jon made an appointment with his solicitor.

I kept my head down and focused on my work. Maria's job was going well and she had managed to save just under four thousand pounds. I worked out our financial position in light of the building delay, and it turned out that if we kept up the good work by the time we'd have thirty-four thousand by the time we started the build. Jon confirmed that this amount would definitely be enough to make the house watertight.

*

The months passed, and the summer warmth was very welcome and took the edge off our uphill struggle. The second week in September marked the start of the build. Jon didn't want us to do the foundations; he employed the experts for that job. While we waited for the foundations to be finished, Jon ordered all the building materials, and I made the arrangements with Edmond for the materials to be stored in the old barn. Once the foundations were finished, we started on the walls, and Jon also employed a bricklayer so things really started to move, and we were getting excited. Jon had managed to secure the mortgage for the farm, ready for when the house had been built and his surveyor thought it best to use the old entrance once the farmhouse and farm were separated. Jon applied for a new entrance to the farmhouse. He also wanted to add greater value to the old farmhouse by giving it a facelift, but Edmond and Sally weren't interested in spending any money. Jon struggled with their decision, but Edmond and Sally were old-school – if it's not broken, don't fix it.

September and October is one of my favourite times of the year. I was working on the house late into the night on most nights. Khan and Jon were there all weekend, from sunrise to sunset. Jon was insisting that the house be watertight before the end of November, which was a tall order.

Working with my brothers could be challenging some-times because once their minds are focused on the job at hand, they will not stop until the job is done. For me, the demands of working the two jobs and trying to build a house and living out in the tent were starting to really show on me. Edmond would often watch me work, sometimes lending a hand, and one night he walked over to me and said, 'I want you to move into our spare room. You're working too hard, and if you're not careful you'll be in hospital soon.'

I knew Edmond was right. I had been coughing for two weeks. I Thanked Edmond for his concern and asked if I could stay with them at weekends. That would give me a little more time for sleeping. Before we started on the house I would visit Maria at weekends so that was a great help. A solid roof over my head two nights a week had been like my medicine, but by that point, I wasn't taking the medicine, because I needed to work every weekend on the house. It was beginning to show.

Edmond had a look of relief on his face. 'Good. Because the farm and this house will be no good to you if you're dead.'

I was shocked by this. Just how bad did I look? Jon and Khan had told me I was doing too much; Khan told me I should drop my plumbing job now – but I couldn't; I wanted our house to be as nice as possible for Maria, and that was my drive. I longed to be back together with Maria in our own place.

The first night I stayed with Edmond and Sally, my cough had intensified and I couldn't stop coughing. Sally was really concerned and suggested that I needed to see a doctor.

'No, a good night's sleep should sort me out hopefully,' I replied, gesturing for her to put the phone away.

I'd be told later how the next morning I just didn't wake up. I was breathing, but I was unresponsive, so Sally called for an ambulance, and I was taken to hospital. After about four days in hospital, I came round. I lay in bed being fed by an intravenous drip, and I was hooked up to oxygen. As I woke up I had no idea what had happened or how long I had been there. I pulled myself up and pressed the emergency button. Within ten minutes a nurse arrived.

'You were admitted Sunday morning,' she explained, 'so you've been here for three and half days. You're suffering from pneumonia.'

'How long will I need to be here?'

'That's a question for the doctor.' Then she told me about how my family had been in to see me lots; that made me feel better, but the only thing I could think about was getting out of the hospital. I had so much work to do, and lying in this bed was driving me mad.

After my conversation with the nurse, I came over very tired and fell asleep again. The next time I woke up, Maria and Aunt Josephine were sitting beside the bed, looking at me. Both of them looked relieved when I opened my eyes.

'It's about time you woke up,' said Josephine. 'We've been so worried about you.' She squeezed my hand, then stood up. 'I'll get us all a cup of tea.'

Maria scooted her chair even closer to my bed and grasped my hand. 'Sean, I'm so glad that you've come round. I've been going out of my mind with worry.' She leant forward. 'Now, listen. I have something to tell you.'

'Is everything okay? With the house?'

'Yes, Sean. Everything's fine. Jon and Khan have been working on the house every day.'

That was music to my ears. Then I realised that we were midway through the week. 'What are they doing about work?'

'Khan's had a week off, and Jon ... well, he must have worked something out as he's also been there every day.'

I puffed out a sigh of relief and sunk back down into my pillow again. I was really lucky to have my family.

Maria looked straight at me and tapped my hand to get my attention again. 'Hey, I've got something that I need to tell you.' By the tone of her voice, I knew it was serious. I turned my head to look straight at Maria and waited.

'The last couple of days have been difficult, to say the least. I was struggling to cope.' I could see her eyes filling up with tears. With effort, I lifted my arm and placed it on her shoulder. 'I'll be out of here soon,' I said.

'Yes, I know you're going to be okay once you get plenty of rest. But the first few days the doctors were very concerned, and I panicked.'

'Well, that's to be expected. But I'll be back to normal in no time.'

'Yes. But Sean, I have something to tell you.'

'Yes, sorry, I'm all ears.'

'We're going to have a baby.'

I was shocked. 'Please can you say that again?'

Maria smiled and repeated herself.

'Again!'

'We're going to have a baby!' she shrieked, then laughed.

'How about you though?' I asked her. 'Are you okay?

'I'm fine, and the baby's fine. Once you were taken into hospital, to be honest, I thought the worst. So I told the family.'

'Well, that's nothing to worry about.'

'I wanted to leave off telling you until the house was watertight. But in all my worry I needed their support, and I felt it was only right that they should know.'

The happiness was bubbling up inside me. I wanted to get out of bed and wrap my arms around her, but I couldn't. Then a thought came to me. 'Maria, could you get your dad over here?'

Maria looked puzzled. 'Why would you want him to visit you?'

I smiled. 'You'll see.'

Just then, Josephine came back with a cup of tea for us all, and a big smile on her face. She took hold of my hand, looked at Maria and said, 'I'm really happy for you both. Congratulations.' Then she turned to me and said, 'Once you get your strength back, I don't want you working so hard. Especially with the baby on the way, Maria is going to need your full support. Also, I think you should move out of the hostel and maybe move into the cottage, or you and Maria can move in with me until your house is ready.'

In that moment I was so grateful to Edmond and Sally for not giving away my homeless status. I agreed with Josephine; I knew that after this episode I didn't want to live rough if I had other choices.

Then Maria came up with the idea of collecting my belongings from the hostel.

'No need,' I quickly replied. 'I never leave anything in there.' Then I changed the subject in case I put my foot in it.

After a while, I started to feel tired. When Maria and

178

Josephine noticed this, they decided it was time to leave, I felt sad as if a piece of me was leaving and I looked at Maria and thought to myself, a piece of me is leaving. I felt like I needed to watch over Maria's every move now, but of course, that wasn't possible at that time as I needed complete rest.

The next day I saw the doctor, and I asked her how much longer I'd need to stay.

'What you need to realise, she said, taking her glasses off to look me in the eye, 'is that you were very lucky that you got to the hospital when you did. I recommend at least a week – and plenty of rest afterwards, unless you want to end up back here.'

That was me told. I'd been lucky, she said, but I felt unlucky at the same time. 'Will I make a full recovery?'

'Yes – if you do as you're told,' she said sternly, but with the hint of a smile on her face.

'What's the recovery time for pneumonia?'

'Six to twelve months – but only if you rest properly.'

Rest was the last thing on my mind, but in my heart, I knew I'd never recover fully if I didn't follow the doctor's instructions.

Later that day, Alex arrived. I was pleased to see him – not least because I found sitting in the hospital so boring, and being still just didn't suit me.

Alex congratulated me, and I could see he was delighted.

'I do hope this means you'll move into the cottage with Maria now until your farmhouse is built. Oh, and congratulations on the farm while I'm at it. You've really turned everything around. Josephine and your family are very proud of you, and even I feel very proud of you, if you don't mind me saying.'

I smiled and thanked Alex.

'He nodded briefly. 'But anyway, Maria told me that you wanted to see me, so what can I do for you?' He sat down.

'That's right. I have something to ask you.' For some reason, I felt very nervous – so nervous that I was shaking.

Alex noticed this. 'Can I get you another blanket?'

'Thanks – but no. I'll be fine. Thank you. Alex, I want to ask you, can I have Maria's hand in marriage?'

Alex looked shocked and there wasn't an immediate reply, which made me feel uncomfortable, especially knowing that Maria was carrying our first child.

Then Alex stood up. He reached out, shook my hand, and replied, 'There isn't anybody in the world that I would rather Maria marry than you.' I felt like I could walk on water; I was so excited. Alex went on, 'You're a good strong man with more determination than I could ever have imagined, and I'm sure you will both be very happy together.' Then he paused. 'Have you asked Maria yet?'

'No, not yet. I wanted to speak to you first. I would've liked to buy Maria a ring, but I think that may well have to wait, because I want to be married before the baby's born.'

'I believe that's the right thing to do. And don't be worrying about a ring. You have enough on your plate,' Alex replied. 'Material things are not important. Honour and respect are much more important, and you're fluent in them. You're a true gentleman.'

We talked some more, and I told Alex about my plans for the farm, and how in the future I wanted to use the farm to help people who find themselves in halfway houses or financial difficulties, the same as me. 'But I will only be able to help people who truly want to help themselves,' I explained. 'That's how I would like it to work. The farm is really hard work, so it wouldn't be any use to anyone who doesn't have a good work ethic.'

Later that same day, my sisters visited me. I was pleased to see them, and they were very excited about Maria expecting. May and Jeff had finally come to an end, and secretly I was pleased about that. Vy had managed to secure a good job with a big law firm, plus she was also chatting to a fellow named Lewis, a defence lawyer, and he sounded interesting, and I joked with Vy that we wouldn't be stuck for legal advice if they became an item. May was now working full-time at the flower shop, and she'd managed to secure two contracts to supply flowers to two very nice hotels.

I told my sisters that I planned to ask Maria to marry me, and they were delighted. They both offered help with getting the house ready, and I laughed, telling them I was writing them each a list of tasks.

*

The next day Maria and Tom came to see me. Maria was glowing – I hadn't been awake enough to notice it the other day – and when I looked at her I felt so happy that my eyes filled up, and my stomach was teeming with butterflies, touching my every sensation and turning it into desire. Maria was everything I wanted and more.

Tom asked me how I was feeling.

'I'm much better today thank you. I should be discharged by the end of the week.'

'Oh, that's great. Will you be coming back to the cottage?'

I replied, 'Yes. I need to be with Maria now. I'm glad you're here, Tom, because I have a very important question I need to ask Maria.'

Maria looked at me slightly puzzled. 'And what is that?'

I said nothing, and managed to haul myself out of bed.

'What are you doing?' Maria asked.

The effort had left me breathless. 'Just ... give me a minute to compose myself,' I managed.

With Tom's help, I got on my knees, and of course, by then Maria had realised what was going on, and she was nervously laughing.

I held her hand and looked up at her. 'Maria, will you do me the greatest honour and be my wife?'

Maria started crying. She wrapped her arms around me and said, 'Only if you promise to always love me the way you do right now.'

'I will,' I murmured.

'Oh, I can't believe this!' Tom cried. 'Congratulations. I'm so happy for you both.' He helped me to my feet, shook my hand and hugged Maria. 'I never expected that. Well done. I feel very excited for you both.'

I told Maria that I want us to be married before the baby is born in March.

Maria asked me, 'Is that why you wanted to speak to my father?'

'Yes. I asked him for your hand in marriage, and he gave me his blessing. So you're going to need a new dress.'

Maria said, 'I cannot think straight. My head feels like it's spinning so fast that I cannot feel my feet.'

Tom said to Maria, 'It's best to let your brain absorb everything first before you make any plans.'

I felt very pleased and content with myself.

After ten days in hospital, I was finally able to leave, and Khan came to pick me up. I planned to have two more weeks of rest at the cottage before I started work again, but before I started my rest I wanted Khan to take me to the farm so that I could see the house.

Khan was right on time as always. I was pleased to see him, and the first thing he did was congratulate me. Once we were in the car Khan said, 'Now, look, I'm sorry I haven't been to see you, but out of concern for your health Edmond took me and Jon to show us where you've been living.'

For some reason hearing this news made me feel sick.

Khan carried on, 'But don't worry, we haven't told Mother, or Vy and May.'

I felt a sense of relief upon hearing that.

'Sean, what were you thinking?' Khan exploded. 'Imagine what would have happened to you if you'd been sleeping in the tent the night you took ill. You were lucky not to lose your life.'

I remained silent.

'Edmond and Sally were in terrible shock after that night. You could have died, and I believe if that night had been spent in the tent, you would have been dead before we found you.'

That thought had never entered my head until now. I suddenly understood my brother's annoyed tone of voice. I told Khan, Yes, you're right. And I understand your concern. But you are not me. It was something that I needed to do – not because I had nowhere else to go but because I wanted to learn how hard it can be. And once I get organised with the farm and the house is finished, I intend to turn the farm into a kind of project, as well as a working farm, for ex-military who find themselves in financial trouble and have nowhere to turn. I needed this experience. I didn't plan this. I just had this driving ambition inside me. I followed my instincts and this is where it brought me. And now I've realised what it was all for – this reason. So please, Khan, try and understand. I wasn't trying to offend anyone.'

Khan looked at me and said, 'I guess I understand, when you put it like that. But I must tell you, Jon was devastated when he saw your tent. In fact, Jon was that upset he's been and taken the tent down and packed it all away so that you can't return.'

'Yeah, that's why I couldn't tell any of you, because I knew this would be the reaction. I did everything possible for you to not find out. I assure you I'm not going to be homeless ever again. Twice in one life is more than enough.'

As we arrived at the house I couldn't believe my eyes. They were putting the roof on. Jon came straight over to the car and as I got out he wrapped his arms around me so tightly and said, 'No more tent.'

'Not if you've got anything to do with it,' I replied. He released me from his hug, and we smiled at each other.

'How have you managed to get so much done?' I asked Khan and Jon.

'Organisation and hard work can get us almost anywhere,' Jon said.

*

After I'd had all the rest I needed, I returned to work at the farm, but I handed in my notice at the plumbing job, due to ill health, and thankfully they accepted it.

When I returned to the farm Edmond and Sally were very pleased to see me, although for several months they wouldn't let me do much. The first thing Edmond said to me was 'I hope you didn't mind me showing your brothers where you were living.'

I shook my head. 'No. You did the right thing. I would have done the same thing if I'd been you.'

'Thank you.' Edmond smiled with relief.

I asked Edmond and Sally if I could stay with them at

the weekend until I get the house finished, and they were thrilled at the suggestion. Then I told them all my good news and invited them to the wedding, which by then was only six weeks away. Last of all, I thanked them both for everything they did on the day I took ill.

Maria was busy planning the wedding and organising the kitchen and bathroom to be fitted. She didn't want a big wedding, just family only and a reception at the estate. Because of the modest wedding, Alex offered to help furnish the house as a wedding present. Maria gladly accepted and I was very relieved about that because once the heating and kitchen and bathroom were done, we could move in. Bedrooms are easy and relatively cheap to install.

The wedding day seemed to come around pretty quickly. May was doing the flowers. Indiana and Nevada were going to be our bridesmaids, and Alexandra and Marcus were going to be the pageboys. My brothers and Tom were to be the ushers. Shannon had booked her flight over from Los Angeles. Willow, Martha and Tam were in charge of the three-course meal. We had managed to find an excellent DJ, Mark Lewis, who was happy to be with us throughout the day. We had thirty guests, made up of family and close friends. We'd booked the little church just outside the estate, which was within easy walking distance. All our plans for the wedding came together beautifully.

The wedding day finally arrived, and for some reason I felt nervous. I made my way to the church, where May had done a beautiful job with the flowers in the church. The vicar was waiting patiently and the choir was doing some last-minute practice. The sun was shining and warm, not a cloud in the sky – it was the most perfect day.

The guests started to arrive, and it felt like ages, waiting for everyone to take their seats, then waiting some more. But eventually, the music started up, and Maria walked in. I turned around and stared. She looked beautiful. The dress was stunning, and her little bump was just starting to show, which in my opinion really suited her. I was a very lucky man, and I knew it. Alex looked very proud, walking his daughter down the aisle. That moment will be engraved in my mind forever.

An hour later, Maria and I walked back down the aisle and I felt very proud and honoured. The doors of the church were open, and the sun rays were shining through the doors. This was a new start, our future together as man and wife.

After the ceremony, we all walked back to the house, and as we were just about to enter the grand old Monmouth suite I recalled my thoughts the last time I entered that very room – about how I'd pictured Maria and me on our wedding day, surrounded by loved ones.

And that's exactly how it went. Maria and I stood outside, waiting to be welcomed in, and then we walked towards the grand dining room where the toastmaster announces us, and we walked through the grand doors, and everybody stands and claps and cheers us into the room. The moment is filled with such love and happiness.

Maria and I turn to look at each other with such admiration and devotion for each other, with a bond so strong that no one can divide us. A love so strong it's eternal.

I guess now I have to admit I'm such a romantic. But sometimes dreams really do come true.

*

Several months after the wedding we finally moved into our new home, and I carried Maria over the threshold. Sitting on the kitchen counter was a fluffy brown teddy bear wearing a military-style top, and Maria raised an eyebrow at me, then walked over to it.

'Oh, Sean. He's beautiful. Is it for the baby?'

I came up behind her, reaching my hands around to the bump. 'Well, yes. But it's for you. And me too, really.'

She turned the bear over, revealing a paper tag. It read:

We will never again be homeless bears.

Epilogue:
Ten Years Later

⚮

Imanaged to get my project off the ground with help and support from various charities. The council gave planning permission for four container pods which could serve as accommodation, and as planned, they are used to help ex-military who find themselves in financial difficulties, just like I once did.

We have three children: Josephine is the oldest, then Len, and then the baby of our bunch is little Sean.

If anybody asked me for advice I would tell them the only thing I understand is work! That gave me the much-needed ability to focus. Without having something to focus on I wouldn't have gotten through.

Maria and my family were amazing, and I understand that's not the same for everyone. That's what gave me the idea for the project. In the beginning, I felt like a total failure in every sense of the word. Accepting help would have made me feel like a bigger failure – although I asked for help when it came to buying the farm and building the house because I know I didn't have a hope in hell of sorting that out without my brothers. In my opinion, to not accept help in certain circumstances becomes foolish. And as tough as I am, and stubborn as I can be, I've never been a fool.

Not only have I put myself back on the map but I now have the means to help others who find themselves in unforeseen circumstances.

For me, work was the key that set me free.

THE END

Ingram Content Group UK Ltd.
Milton Keynes UK
UKHW040952220523
422012UK00012B/2

9 781913 460525